CONNECTED MATHEMATICS

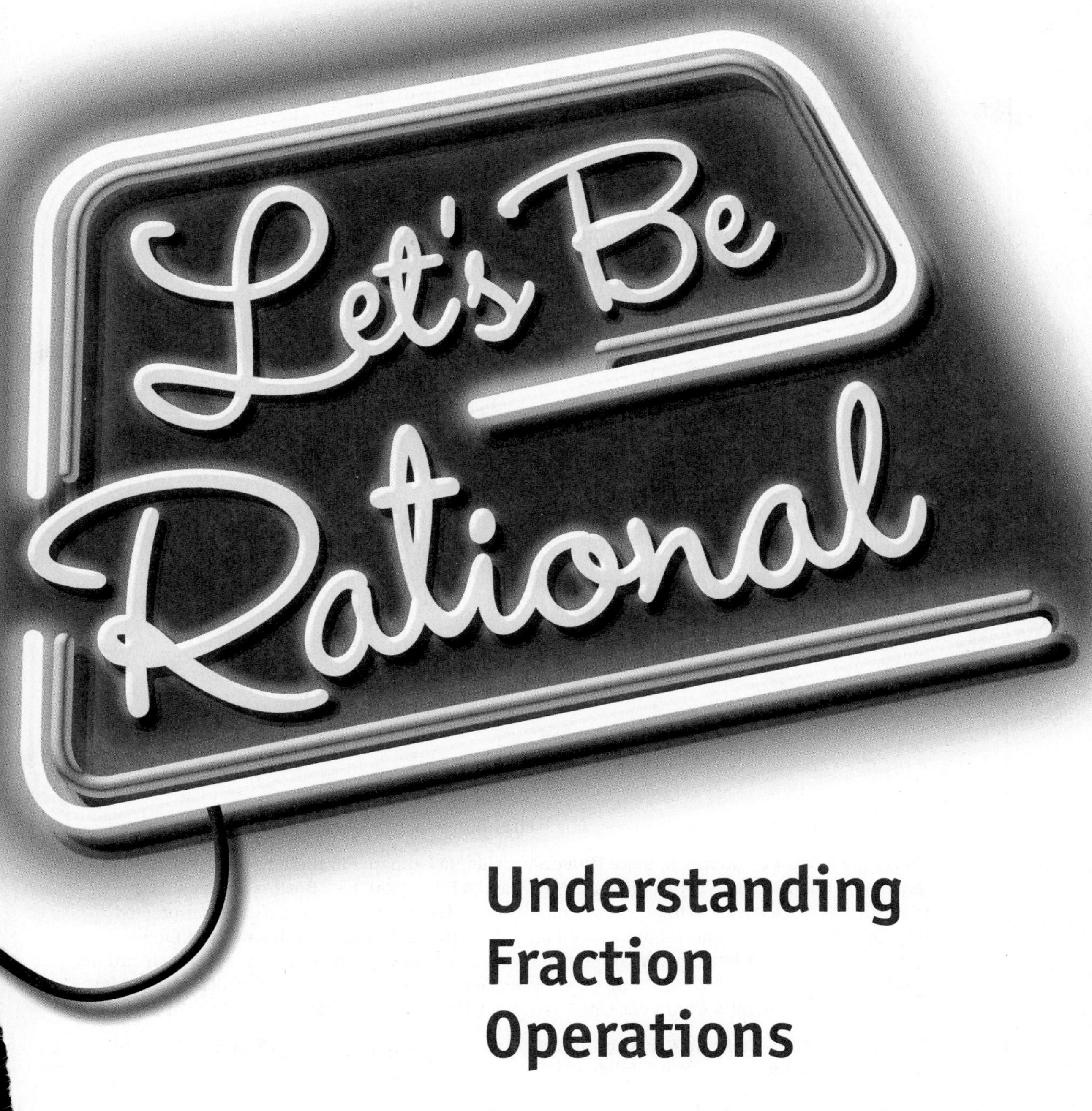

Understanding Fraction Operations

Glenda Lappan, Elizabeth Difanis Phillips,
James T. Fey, Susan N. Friel

PEARSON

sachusetts • Chandler, Arizona • Glenview, Illinois • Upper Saddle River, New Jersey

Connected Mathematics® was developed at Michigan State University with financial support from the Michigan State University Office of the Provost, Computing and Technology, and the College of Natural Science.

This material is based upon work supported by the National Science Foundation under Grant No. MDR 9150217 and Grant No. ESI 9986372. Opinions expressed are those of the authors and not necessarily those of the Foundation.

As with prior editions of this work, the authors and administration of Michigan State University preserve a tradition of devoting royalties from this publication to support activities sponsored by the MSU Mathematics Education Enrichment Fund.

Acknowledgments appear on page 88, which constitutes an extension of this copyright page.

PEARSON

13-digit ISBN 978-0-13-32744
10-digit ISBN 0-13-32744
4 5 6 7 8 9 10 V011 17 16 15 1

Authors

A Team of Experts

Glenda Lappan is a University Distinguished Professor in the Program in Mathematics Education (PRIME) and the Department of Mathematics at Michigan State University. Her research and development interests are in the connected areas of students' learning of mathematics and mathematics teachers' professional growth and change related to the development and enactment of K–12 curriculum materials.

Elizabeth Difanis Phillips is a Senior Academic Specialist in the Program in Mathematics Education (PRIME) and the Department of Mathematics at Michigan State University. She is interested in teaching and learning mathematics for both teachers and students. These interests have led to curriculum and professional development projects at the middle school and high school levels, as well as projects related to the teaching and learning of algebra across the grades.

James T. Fey is a Professor Emeritus at the University of Maryland. His consistent professional interest has been development and research focused on curriculum materials that engage middle and high school students in problem-based collaborative investigations of mathematical ideas and their applications.

Susan N. Friel is a Professor of Mathematics Education in the School of Education at the University of North Carolina at Chapel Hill. Her research interests focus on statistics education for middle-grade students and, more broadly, on teachers' professional development and growth in teaching mathematics K–8.

With... Yvonne Grant and Jacqueline Stewart

Yvonne Grant teaches mathematics at Portland Middle School in Portland, Michigan. Jacqueline Stewart is a recently retired high school teacher of mathematics at Okemos High School in Okemos, Michigan. Both Yvonne and Jacqueline have worked on a variety of activities related to the development, implementation, and professional development of the CMP curriculum since its beginning in 1991.

Development Team

CMP3 Authors

Glenda Lappan, University Distinguished Professor, Michigan State University
Elizabeth Difanis Phillips, Senior Academic Specialist, Michigan State University
James T. Fey, Professor Emeritus, University of Maryland
Susan N. Friel, Professor, University of North Carolina – Chapel Hill

With...

Yvonne Grant, Portland Middle School, Michigan
Jacqueline Stewart, Mathematics Consultant, Mason, Michigan

In Memory of... William M. Fitzgerald, Professor (Deceased), Michigan State University, who made substantial contributions to conceptualizing and creating CMP1.

Administrative Assistant

Michigan State University
Judith Martus Miller

Support Staff

Michigan State University
Undergraduate Assistants:
Bradley Robert Corlett, Carly Fleming, Erin Lucian, Scooter Nowak

Development Assistants

Michigan State University
Graduate Research Assistants:
Richard "Abe" Edwards, Nic Gilbertson, Funda Gonulates, Aladar Horvath, Eun Mi Kim, Kevin Lawrence, Jennifer Nimtz, Joanne Philhower, Sasha Wang

Assessment Team

Maine

Falmouth Public Schools
Falmouth Middle School: Shawn Towle

Michigan

Ann Arbor Public Schools
Tappan Middle School
Anne Marie Nicoll-Turner

Portland Public Schools
Portland Middle School
Holly DeRosia, Yvonne Grant

Traverse City Area Public Schools
Traverse City East Middle School
Jane Porath, Mary Beth Schmitt

Traverse City West Middle School
Jennifer Rundio, Karrie Tufts

Ohio

Clark-Shawnee Local Schools
Rockway Middle School: Jim Mamer

Content Consultants

Michigan State University
Peter Lappan, Professor Emeritus, Department of Mathematics

Normandale Community College
Christopher Danielson, Instructor, Department of Mathematics & Statistics

University of North Carolina – Wilmington
Dargan Frierson, Jr., Professor, Department of Mathematics & Statistics

Student Activities

Michigan State University
Brin Keller, Associate Professor, Department of Mathematics

Consultants

Indiana

Purdue University
Mary Bouck, Mathematics Consultant

Michigan

Oakland Schools
Valerie Mills, Mathematics Education Supervisor
Mathematics Education Consultants: Geraldine Devine, Dana Gosen

Ellen Bacon, Independent Mathematics Consultant

New York

University of Rochester
Jeffrey Choppin, Associate Professor

Ohio

University of Toledo
Debra Johanning, Associate Professor

Pennsylvania

University of Pittsburgh
Margaret Smith, Professor

Texas

University of Texas at Austin
Emma Trevino, Supervisor of Mathematics Programs, The Dana Center

Mathematics for All Consulting
Carmen Whitman, Mathematics Consultant

Reviewers

Michigan

Ionia Public Schools
Kathy Dole, Director of Curriculum and Instruction

Grand Valley State University
Lisa Kasmer, Assistant Professor

Portland Public Schools
Teri Keusch, Classroom Teacher

Minnesota

Hopkins School District 270
Michele Luke, Mathematics Coordinator

Field Test Sites for CMP3

Michigan

Ann Arbor Public Schools
Tappan Middle School
Anne Marie Nicoll-Turner*

Portland Public Schools
Portland Middle School: Mark Braun, Angela Buckland, Holly DeRosia, Holly Feldpausch, Angela Foote, Yvonne Grant*, Kristin Roberts, Angie Stump, Tammi Wardwell

Traverse City Area Public Schools
Traverse City East Middle School
Ivanka Baic Berkshire, Brenda Dunscombe, Tracie Herzberg, Deb Larimer, Jan Palkowski, Rebecca Perreault, Jane Porath*, Robert Sagan, Mary Beth Schmitt*

Traverse City West Middle School
Pamela Alfieri, Jennifer Rundio, Maria Taplin, Karrie Tufts*

Maine

Falmouth Public Schools
Falmouth Middle School: Sally Bennett, Chris Driscoll, Sara Jones, Shawn Towle*

Minnesota

Minneapolis Public Schools
Jefferson Community School
Leif Carlson*,
Katrina Hayek Munsisoumang*

Ohio

Clark-Shawnee Local Schools
Reid School: Joanne Gilley
Rockway Middle School: Jim Mamer*
Possum School: Tami Thomas

*Indicates a Field Test Site Coordinator

Let's Be Rational

Understanding Fraction Operations

3 Dividing With Fractions

4 Wrapping Up the Operations

Looking Ahead

Min Ji has a $\frac{7}{8}$-yard strip of balsa wood. Shawn wants to buy half of the balsa wood. **How long** is the strip of wood Shawn wants to buy?

There are 12 rabbits at a pet store. Gabriella has $5\frac{1}{2}$ ounces of parsley to feed the rabbits. **How much** parsley does each rabbit get?

Jimarcus plans to build a fence at the back of his garden. If the fence will be $5\frac{1}{3}$ yards long, **how many** $\frac{2}{3}$-yard sections of fence will he need?

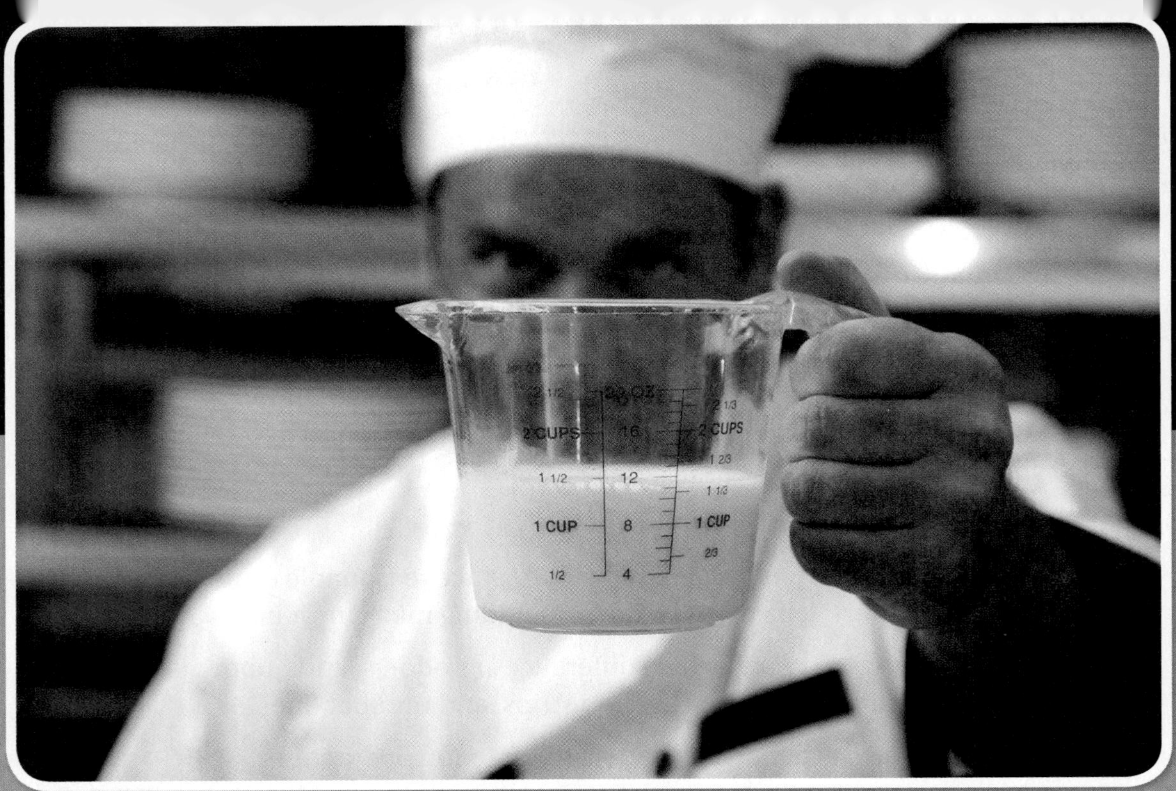

In *Comparing Bits and Pieces*, you learned what fractions, decimals, ratios, and percents mean. You also explored different real-world situations in which these numbers are used.

In *Let's Be Rational*, you will investigate situations such as those described on the previous page. These situations require addition, subtraction, multiplication, or division of fractions, including mixed numbers. You will decide which operation makes sense in each situation.

Knowing strategies for working with all kinds of numbers is very important. If you take part in developing these strategies, they will make more sense to you. You will be able to more easily apply these strategies to other situations.

You may already know some shortcuts for working with fractions. During this Unit, you will think about why those shortcuts, and the strategies you develop with your class, make sense. Remember, it is not enough to answer a problem. The real power is your ability to discuss your ideas and strategies and use them in new situations.

Mathematical Highlights

Understanding Fraction Operations

In *Let's Be Rational,* you will develop an understanding of the four basic arithmetic operations with fractions, including mixed numbers. You will also describe strategies for using these operations when solving problems involving fractions.

You will learn how to

- Use benchmarks and other strategies to make reasonable estimates for results of operations with fractions, including mixed numbers
- Develop ways to model sums, differences, products, and quotients, including the use of areas, fraction strips, and number lines
- Look for rules to generalize patterns in fraction operations
- Use your knowledge of fractions, equivalence of fractions, and properties of numbers to develop algorithms for adding, subtracting, multiplying, and dividing fractions
- Recognize when addition, subtraction, multiplication, or division is the appropriate operation to solve a problem
- Write fact families to show the inverse relationship between addition and subtraction, and between multiplication and division
- Solve problems using operations on fractions, including mixed numbers
- Find values for variables by using operations on fractions, including mixed numbers

When you encounter a new problem, it is a good idea to ask yourself questions. In this Unit, you might ask questions such as:

What models or diagrams might be helpful in understanding the problem situation and the relationships among quantities?

What models or diagrams might help you decide which operation is useful in solving a problem?

What is a reasonable estimate for the answer?

Common Core State Standards

Mathematical Practices and Habits of Mind

In the *Connected Mathematics* curriculum you will develop an understanding of important mathematical ideas by solving problems and reflecting on the mathematics involved. Every day, you will use "habits of mind" to make sense of problems and apply what you learn to new situations. Some of these habits are described by the *Common Core State Standards for Mathematical Practices* (MP).

MP1 Make sense of problems and persevere in solving them.

When using mathematics to solve a problem, it helps to think carefully about

- data and other facts you are given and what additional information you need to solve the problem;
- strategies you have used to solve similar problems and whether you could solve a related simpler problem first;
- how you could express the problem with equations, diagrams, or graphs;
- whether your answer makes sense.

MP2 Reason abstractly and quantitatively.

When you are asked to solve a problem, it often helps to

- focus first on the key mathematical ideas;
- check that your answer makes sense in the problem setting;
- use what you know about the problem setting to guide your mathematical reasoning.

MP3 Construct viable arguments and critique the reasoning of others.

When you are asked to explain why a conjecture is correct, you can

- show some examples that fit the claim and explain why they fit;
- show how a new result follows logically from known facts and principles.

When you believe a mathematical claim is incorrect, you can

- show one or more counterexamples—cases that don't fit the claim;
- find steps in the argument that do not follow logically from prior claims.

MP4 Model with mathematics.

When you are asked to solve problems, it often helps to

- think carefully about the numbers or geometric shapes that are the most important factors in the problem, then ask yourself how those factors are related to each other;
- express data and relationships in the problem with tables, graphs, diagrams, or equations, and check your result to see if it makes sense.

MP5 Use appropriate tools strategically.

When working on mathematical questions, you should always

- decide which tools are most helpful for solving the problem and why;
- try a different tool when you get stuck.

MP6 Attend to precision.

In every mathematical exploration or problem-solving task, it is important to

- think carefully about the required accuracy of results; is a number estimate or geometric sketch good enough, or is a precise value or drawing needed?
- report your discoveries with clear and correct mathematical language that can be understood by those to whom you are speaking or writing.

MP7 Look for and make use of structure.

In mathematical explorations and problem solving, it is often helpful to

- look for patterns that show how data points, numbers, or geometric shapes are related to each other;
- use patterns to make predictions.

MP8 Look for and express regularity in repeated reasoning.

When results of a repeated calculation show a pattern, it helps to

- express that pattern as a general rule that can be used in similar cases;
- look for shortcuts that will make the calculation simpler in other cases.

You will use all of the Mathematical Practices in this Unit. Sometimes, when you look at a Problem, it is obvious which practice is most helpful. At other times, you will decide on a practice to use during class explorations and discussions. After completing each Problem, ask yourself:

- What mathematics have I learned by solving this Problem?
- What Mathematical Practices were helpful in learning this mathematics?

Extending Addition and Subtraction of Fractions

Knowing how to combine and separate quantities is helpful in understanding the world around you. The mathematical names for combining and separating quantities are *adding* and *subtracting*. The result of addition is called a *sum*; the result of subtraction is called a *difference*.

Sometimes when you need to find a sum or difference, you do not need an exact answer. In these situations, making a reasonable estimate is good enough. It is *always* a good idea to estimate, even when you want an exact answer. You can check your exact answer by comparing it to an estimate.

- What is a good estimate for 198 + 605?
- What is a good estimate for 7.9 − 1.04?
- How do these estimates help you check the exact sum and difference?

Common Core State Standards

6.NS.B.4 Find the greatest common factor of two whole numbers less than or equal to 100 and the least common multiple of two whole numbers less than or equal to 12. . .

6.EE.B.7 Solve real-world and mathematical problems by writing and solving equations of the form $x + p = q$ and $px = q$ for cases in which p, q and x are all nonnegative rational numbers.

Also 6.EE.A.2, 6.EE.A.2b, 6.EE.B.5, 6.EE.B.6

1.1 Getting Close
Estimating Sums

Getting Close is a game that will sharpen your estimating skills by using **benchmarks.** A benchmark is a reference number that can be used to estimate the size of other numbers. Examine this set of benchmarks.

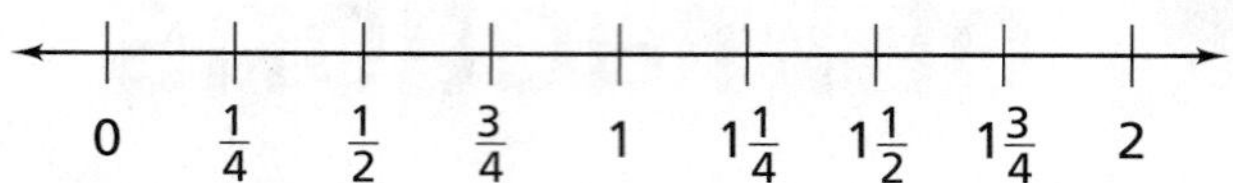

- Which fraction benchmark is $\frac{3}{8}$ closest to?

Raul says that $\frac{3}{8}$ is exactly halfway between $\frac{1}{4}$ and $\frac{1}{2}$. He reasons that $\frac{3}{8}$ is less than $\frac{1}{2}$ because it is less than $\frac{4}{8}$. However, $\frac{3}{8}$ is greater than $\frac{1}{4}$ because it is greater than $\frac{2}{8}$.

- Which benchmark is 0.58 closest to?

Desiree says that since $\frac{1}{2}$ is equal to 0.50, 0.58 is greater than $\frac{1}{2}$. Also, 0.58 is less than 0.75, which equals $\frac{3}{4}$. So 0.58 is between $\frac{1}{2}$ and $\frac{3}{4}$, but it is closer to $\frac{1}{2}$.

- Is Desiree correct?
- Is there another way to find the closest benchmark?

Cetera wonders if she can use benchmarks to estimate the sum of two fractions, such as the sum below.

$$\frac{1}{2} + \frac{5}{8}$$

- Is the sum between 0 and 1 or between 1 and 2?
- Is the sum closest to 0, to 1, or to 2?

You can practice using benchmarks and other strategies to estimate the sum of two numbers during the Getting Close game.

Getting Close Game

Two to four players can play Getting Close.

Materials

- Getting Close fraction or decimal game cards (one set per group)
- A set of four number squares (0, 1, 2, and 3) for each player

Directions

1. All players hold their 0, 1, 2, and 3 number squares in their hand. The game cards are placed facedown in a pile in the center of the table.
2. One player turns over two game cards from the pile. Each player mentally estimates the sum of the numbers on the two game cards.
3. Each player then selects a number square (0, 1, 2, or 3) closest to their estimate and places it facedown on the table.
4. After each player has played a number square, the players turn their number squares over at the same time.
5. Each player calculates the actual sum by hand or with a calculator. The player whose number square is closest to the actual sum gets the two game cards.
   Note: If there is a tie, all players who tied get one game card. Players who have tied may take a game card from the deck if necessary.
6. Players take turns turning over the two game cards.
7. When all game cards have been used, the player with the most game cards wins.

Problem 1.1

Play Getting Close several times. Keep a record of the estimation strategies you find useful. Use these estimation strategies to answer the questions below.

A Suppose you played Getting Close with only these game cards:

$\frac{2}{3}$ $\frac{9}{10}$ $\frac{4}{5}$ $\frac{1}{2}$

1. Which two cards have the greatest sum? How do you know? Estimate the sum.
2. Which two cards have the least sum? How do you know? Estimate the sum.

B Suppose you played Getting Close with only these game cards:

0.25 0.9 0.125 0.75

1. Which two cards have the greatest sum? How do you know? Estimate the sum.
2. Which two cards have the least sum? How do you know? Estimate the sum.

C Suppose you played Getting Close with only these game cards:

$\frac{3}{4}$ 0.25 0.33

1. Which two cards have the greatest sum? The least sum? How do you know? Estimate the greatest sum and the least sum.
2. How can you estimate the sum of two game cards when one game card is a decimal and one game card is a fraction?

D Estimate each sum to the nearest whole number. Explain how you made each estimate.

1. $\frac{2}{3} + \frac{1}{5}$
2. $2\frac{1}{3} + 3\frac{2}{3}$
3. $\frac{3}{4} + \frac{4}{3}$

ACE Homework starts on page 18.

1.2 Estimating Sums and Differences

It is important to know how to find exact sums and differences. It is also important to be able to make good estimates. If an exact answer is not necessary, you can solve problems more quickly by estimating. Estimates help you know whether or not an answer is reasonable.

- What are some situations in which you can estimate a sum or difference instead of finding an exact answer?

Sometimes you should **overestimate,** or give an estimate that is a bit bigger than the actual value. Overestimate to make sure you have enough. Sometimes you should **underestimate,** or give an estimate that is a bit smaller than the actual value. Underestimate to stay below a certain limit.

Problem 1.2

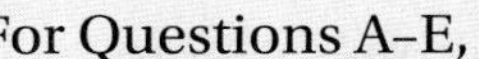

For Questions A–E,

- Answer the question by using estimation. Explain your reasoning.
- Explain how confident you are in your answer.
- For each estimate you make, tell whether it is an overestimate or an underestimate. Explain why you chose to overestimate or underestimate.

A Mrs. Edwards is building a dollhouse for her children. She needs to buy wood for the railing on the balcony.

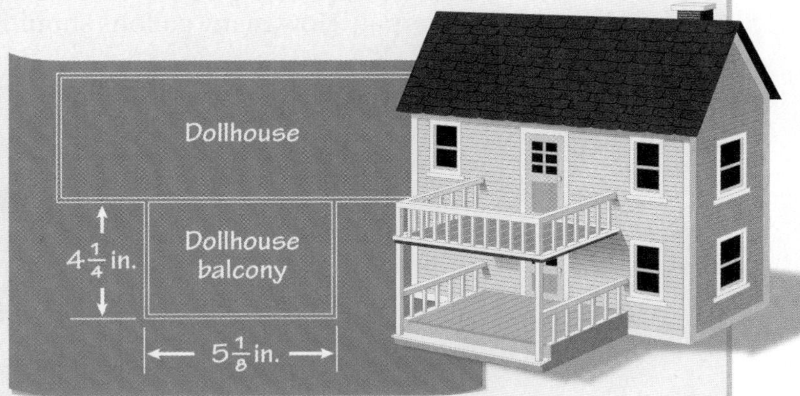

The wood is available in 12-inch, 14-inch, and 16-inch lengths. She does not want to waste wood. What length should she buy?

continued on the next page >

Problem 1.2 continued

B Mr. Cheng is making shades for his office. One window needs $1\frac{1}{3}$ yards of material and the other window needs $1\frac{3}{4}$ yards of material. The fabric store only sells whole-number lengths of this material. How many yards of material should Mr. Cheng buy?

C Mr. Aleman is the treasurer for his local scouting troop. He makes a budget for the troop. He suggests that they spend $\frac{1}{2}$ of their money on field trips, $\frac{1}{3}$ of their money on events, and $\frac{1}{4}$ of their money on scholarships. He wants to save the rest of the troop's money for next year. What do you think of Mr. Aleman's budget?

D Jasmine is making jam to enter in the state fair.

1. Jasmine's raspberry jam recipe calls for $4\frac{1}{3}$ quarts of raspberries. She has picked $3\frac{1}{2}$ quarts of raspberries. About how many more quarts of raspberries should she pick?
2. Jasmine's mixed berry jam recipe calls for $6\frac{2}{3}$ quarts of berries. She has $3\frac{1}{3}$ quarts of strawberries and $2\frac{7}{8}$ quarts of blackberries. Does Jasmine have enough berries? If not, about how many more quarts of berries does she need to pick?

E The gas tank on Priya's pontoon boat can hold 5 gallons. It is completely empty. Priya needs a full tank for the day's activities. She adds $2\frac{1}{4}$ gallons from a gas canister and then takes the boat to a nearby marina to fill it up. She has to pay ahead. Priya wants the tank as full as possible but does not want to overpay. How many gallons should Priya ask for?

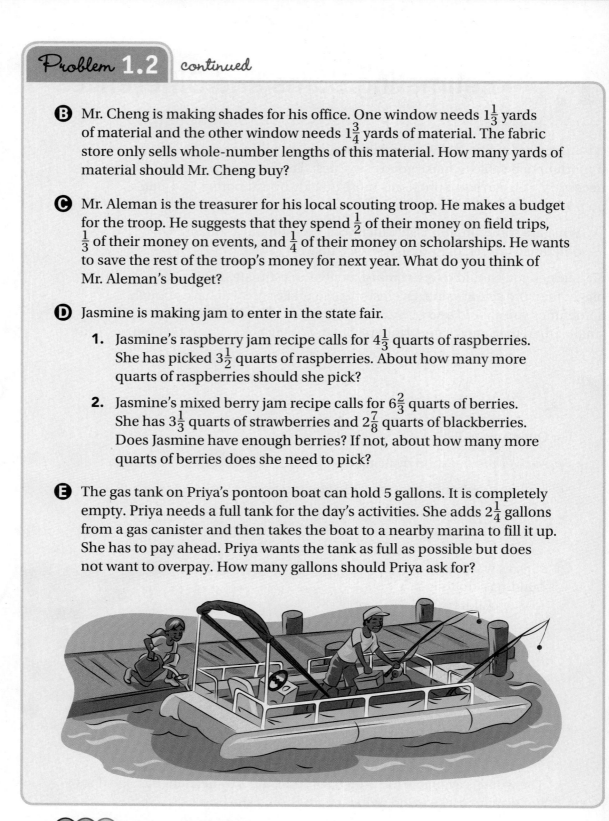

ACE Homework starts on page 18.

1.3 Land Sections

Adding and Subtracting Fractions

When Tupelo Township was founded, the land was divided into sections that could be farmed. Each section is a square that is 1 mile long on each side. In other words, each section is 1 square mile of land. There are 640 acres of land in one square-mile section.

Over time, the owners of the sections have bought and sold land, so each section is owned by several owners. You can use **number sentences** to find how much land each owner has.

If a farmer owns 2 acres of land and buys another $1\frac{1}{2}$ acres of land, she will have $2 + 1\frac{1}{2}$, or $3\frac{1}{2}$, acres of land. The number sentence that shows this relationship is

$$2 + 1\frac{1}{2} = 3\frac{1}{2}$$

The *sum* of the parts is the total land the farmer owns, $3\frac{1}{2}$ acres.

If a farmer has $2\frac{1}{2}$ acres of land and then sells $\frac{1}{2}$ of an acre of land, she will own $2\frac{1}{2} - \frac{1}{2}$, or 2, acres of land. The number sentence that shows this relationship is:

$$2\frac{1}{2} - \frac{1}{2} = 2$$

The *difference* is the land the farmer still owns, 2 acres.

This Problem requires you to add and subtract fractions to find exact answers. Remember to estimate to make sure that your answers are reasonable. As you work, use what you know about fractions and finding *equivalent fractions*. Write number sentences to communicate your strategies for solving the Problem.

The diagram below shows two sections of land that are *adjacent,* or side by side, in Tupelo Township. Several people share ownership of each section. The diagram shows the part of a section each person owns.

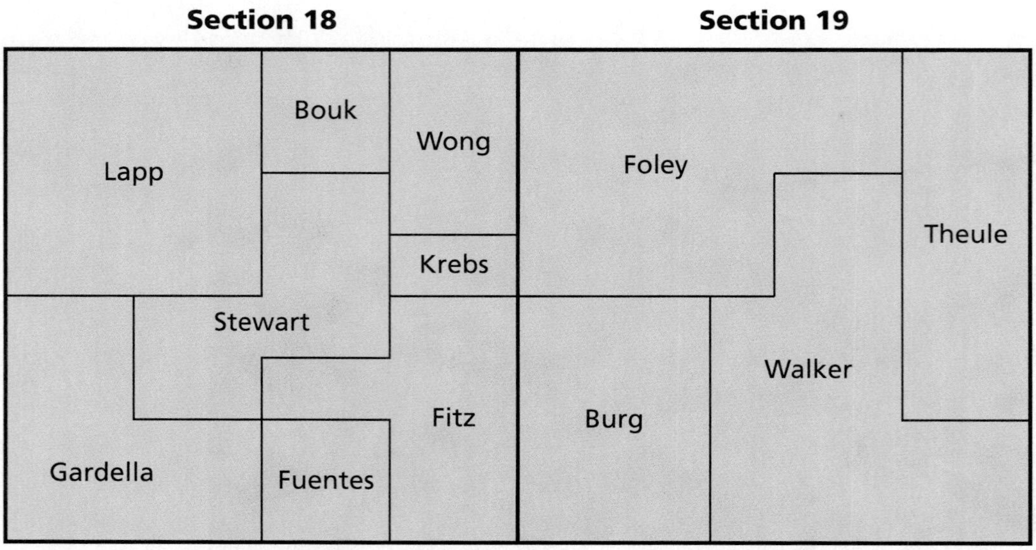

- Who owns the most land in Section 18? In Section 19?

Problem 1.3

A What fraction of a section does each person own? Explain how you know.

For Questions B and C,

- Find an approximate answer using estimation.
- Write a number sentence and answer the question.
- Compare your answer to your estimate to make sure your answer is reasonable.
- Identify the meaning of each number and symbol in your number sentence.

B
1. Stewart and Bouck combine their land. What fraction of a section do they now own together?
2. Foley and Burg combine their land. What fraction of a section do they now own together?
3. How much more land does Lapp own than Wong?

C
1. Name a set of owners whose combined land equals $1\frac{1}{2}$ sections.
2. Name a set of owners whose combined land equals $1\frac{3}{4}$ sections.

D
1. Each section of land is one square mile. One square mile is equal to 640 acres. How many acres of land does each person own? Explain your reasoning.
2. Foley, Walker, Burg, and Krebs sell their land for a state park. How many acres are covered by the state park? Explain.
3. After Foley, Walker, Burg, and Krebs sell their land, what fraction of Section 19 remains in private ownership? Explain.

E
1. Which set of owners' combined land does this number sentence represent?

$$1 + \frac{1}{4} + \frac{3}{16} + \frac{1}{16} = 1\frac{1}{2}$$

2. Explain how you know that this sum of fractions is exactly equal to $1\frac{1}{2}$.

ACE Homework starts on page 18.

1.4 Visiting the Spice Shop

Adding and Subtracting Mixed Numbers

All over the world, cooks use spices to add flavor to foods. Because recipe ingredients are often measured using fractions, cooking can involve operating with fractional quantities.

Reyna owns a spice shop in Tupelo Township. Some of her recipes are shown below.

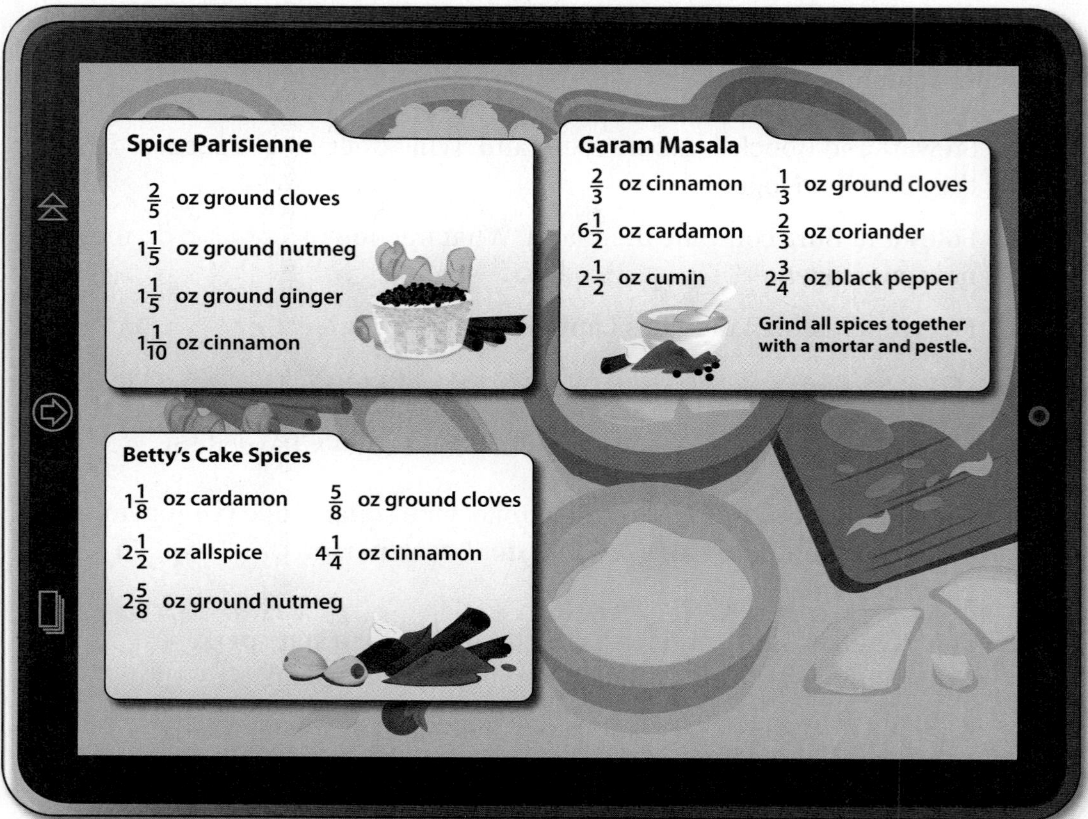

Spice Parisienne
$\frac{2}{5}$ oz ground cloves
$1\frac{1}{5}$ oz ground nutmeg
$1\frac{1}{5}$ oz ground ginger
$1\frac{1}{10}$ oz cinnamon
Garam Masala
$\frac{2}{3}$ oz cinnamon
$6\frac{1}{2}$ oz cardamon
$2\frac{1}{2}$ oz cumin
$\frac{1}{3}$ oz ground cloves
$\frac{2}{3}$ oz coriander
$2\frac{3}{4}$ oz black pepper
Grind all spices together with a mortar and pestle.
Betty's Cake Spices
$1\frac{1}{8}$ oz cardamon
$2\frac{1}{2}$ oz allspice
$2\frac{5}{8}$ oz ground nutmeg
$\frac{5}{8}$ oz ground cloves
$4\frac{1}{4}$ oz cinnamon

- Which makes a greater amount of spice mix, Betty's Cake Spices recipe, or the Garam Masala recipe? How much more spice mix?

Problem 1.4

A 1. Latisha buys spices to make one batch of Spice Parisienne. Use estimation to decide whether she buys more or less than 4 ounces of spices. Explain your reasoning.

2. Use estimation to decide which weighs more, one batch of Betty's Cake Spices or one batch of Garam Masala. About how much more does it weigh? Explain.

For Questions B and C,

- Decide which operation you will use to solve each problem.
- Find an approximate answer using estimation.
- Write a number sentence and answer the question.

B Betty buys spices for her famous cake.

1. How many ounces of spice does Betty buy?
2. Tevin is allergic to cinnamon. If Betty removes cinnamon from the recipe for him, how many ounces of spice does she buy?

C Ms. Garza buys spices to make one batch of Garam Masala. When she weighs her spices at home, she only has $10\frac{11}{12}$ ounces of spice. Which spice did Ms. Garza forget?

D Renuka has two pounds of pepper in her cupboard. She knows that there are 16 ounces in one pound. After Renuka makes one batch of Garam Masala, how many ounces of pepper does Renuka have left in her cupboard?

E For each number sentence below, write a spice story. Then find the value for N that makes the sentence true.

1. $3\frac{1}{6} - 1\frac{3}{4} = N$
2. $N + \frac{3}{4} = 1\frac{1}{2}$
3. $2\frac{2}{3} - N = 1\frac{1}{4}$

F 1. Describe a strategy for estimating sums and differences of fractions, including mixed numbers.

2. An **algorithm** (AL guh rith um) is a plan, or a series of steps, for doing a computation. Each step in an algorithm should be clear and precise. Describe an algorithm for finding sums and differences of fractions, including mixed numbers.

ACE Homework starts on page 18.

Applications

For Exercises 1–6, determine whether the number is closest to 0, $\frac{1}{2}$, or 1. Explain your reasoning.

1. $\frac{10}{9}$
2. $\frac{9}{16}$
3. $\frac{5}{6}$
4. $\frac{48}{100}$
5. 0.67
6. 0.0009999

For Exercises 7–12, determine whether the sum of the two Getting Close game cards is closest to 0, 1, 2, or 3. Explain.

7. $\frac{7}{8}$ and $\frac{4}{9}$
8. $1\frac{3}{4}$ and $\frac{1}{8}$
9. $1\frac{1}{3}$ and 1.3
10. 0.25 and $\frac{1}{8}$
11. 1.352 and 0.84
12. $1\frac{4}{10}$ and 0.375

For Exercises 13–15, you are playing a game called Getting Even Closer. In this game, you have to estimate sums to the nearest $\frac{1}{2}$ or 0.5. Decide if the sum of the two game cards turned up is closest to 0, 0.5, or 1. Explain.

13. $\frac{3}{5}$ $\frac{1}{10}$
14. $\frac{1}{4}$ $\frac{1}{10}$
15. $\frac{1}{9}$ $\frac{1}{8}$

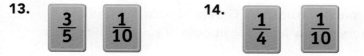

16. Four students were asked the following question: "Can you find two fractions with a sum greater than $\frac{3}{4}$?" Explain whether or not each answer below is correct.
    a. $\frac{1}{8}+\frac{2}{4}$
    b. $\frac{3}{6}+\frac{2}{4}$
    c. $\frac{5}{12}+\frac{5}{6}$
    d. $\frac{5}{10}+\frac{3}{8}$

For Exercises 17–20, find two fractions with a sum that is between the two given numbers.

17. 0 and $\frac{1}{2}$
18. $\frac{1}{2}$ and 1
19. 1 and $1\frac{1}{2}$
20. $1\frac{1}{2}$ and 2

21. A new set of Getting Close Cards contains the following numbers:

$$1.05 \qquad 0.7 \qquad \frac{3}{5} \qquad \frac{1}{4} \qquad \frac{9}{10}$$

a. Which two cards have the greatest sum?

b. Which two cards have the least sum?

22. Julio is at the grocery store. He has $10.00. Here is a list of the items he would like to buy.

12:30 PM
Milk $2.47
Eggs $1.09
Cheese $1.95
Bread $0.68
Honey $1.19
Cereal $3.25
Avocado $0.50
Chipotles $1.29

Use mental computation and estimation to answer parts (a)–(c).

a. Can Julio buy all the items with the money he has? Explain your reasoning.

b. If Julio only has $5.00, what can he buy? Give two possible combinations.

c. What different items can he buy to come as close as possible to spending $5.00?

23. Many sewing patterns have a $\frac{5}{8}$-inch border for sewing the seam. Is a $\frac{5}{8}$-inch border closest to 0, $\frac{1}{2}$, or 1 inch? Explain your reasoning.

24. Soo needs 2 yards of molding to put around the bottom of a stand. He has two pieces of molding. One piece is $\frac{7}{8}$ of a yard long. The other is $\frac{8}{7}$ yards long. Estimate whether or not he has enough molding. Explain.

25. Reggie picked $3\frac{3}{4}$ quarts of blueberries and $4\frac{1}{3}$ quarts of raspberries at a fruit farm. *About* how many total quarts of berries did he pick?

26. You mix $\frac{5}{8}$ of a cup of wheat flour with $1\frac{3}{4}$ cups of white flour. Do you have enough flour for a recipe that calls for $2\frac{1}{2}$ cups of flour? Explain.

27. The Langstons planted a big garden with flowers.

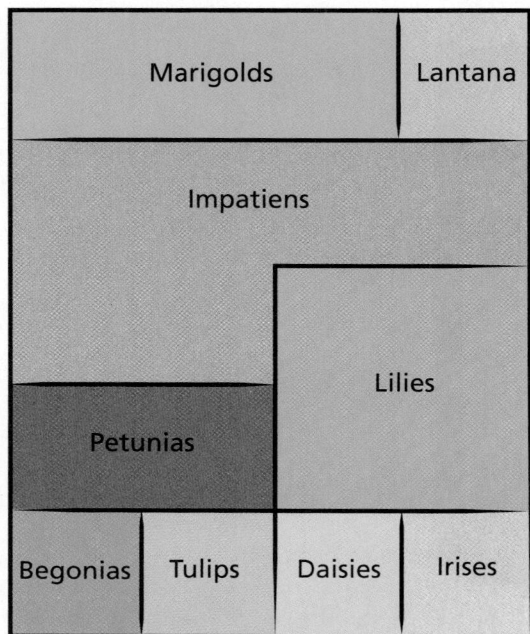

a. About what fraction of the garden is planted with each type of flower?

b. How much more of the garden is planted with lilies than daisies?

c. The Langstons replace the daisies and irises with lilies. What fraction of the garden is planted with lilies? Write a number sentence.

d. In the following sentence, the name of each type of flower represents the fraction of the garden in which the flower is planted.

$$\text{Marigolds} - \text{Begonias} = \text{Petunias} + \text{Tulips}$$

Use fractions to explain whether the sentence is correct or incorrect.

e. Look at the original garden plan. Find three different combinations of plots that total the fraction of the garden planted with impatiens. Write a number sentence for each combination.

For Exercises 28–30, use the sample magazine page shown.

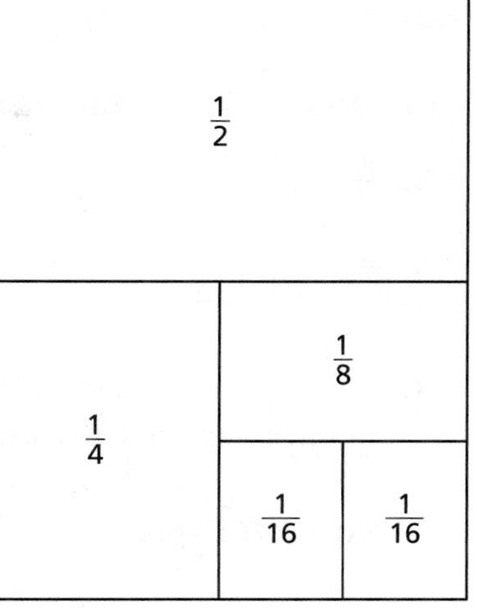

28. A local magazine sells space for ads. It charges advertisers according to the fraction of a page purchased.

a. Advertisers purchase $\frac{1}{8}$ and $\frac{1}{16}$ of page 20. What fraction of the page is used for ads?

b. What fraction of page 20 remains available for other uses? Explain.

29. The Cool Sub Shop is having its grand opening. The owner buys three $\frac{1}{4}$-page ads, four $\frac{1}{8}$-page ads, and ten $\frac{1}{16}$-page ads. What is the total amount of ad space that the owner buys?

30. A local concert promoter purchases $2\frac{3}{4}$ pages of ads. When one of the concerts is canceled, the promoter cancels $1\frac{5}{8}$ pages of ads. How much advertising space is the concert promoter actually using?

31. Rico and his friend eat some lasagna. Rico eats $\frac{1}{9}$ of the lasagna, and his friend eats $\frac{1}{18}$ of the lasagna. How much of the lasagna is left?

32. Sonia finds a $\frac{3}{4}$-full small bag of chips. She eats the rest of the chips in the bag. Then she opens another small bag of chips. Sonia eats $\frac{1}{8}$ of those chips. What fraction of a small bag of chips does Sonia eat altogether?

For Exercises 33–36, find each sum or difference.

33. $1\frac{2}{5} + 1\frac{1}{3}$

34. $2\frac{1}{8} + 3\frac{3}{4} + 1\frac{1}{2}$

35. $11\frac{1}{2} - 2\frac{2}{3}$

36. $8\frac{11}{12} - 2\frac{3}{4}$

For Exercises 37–38, determine which sum or difference is greater. Show your work.

37. $\frac{2}{3} + \frac{5}{6}$ or $\frac{3}{4} + \frac{4}{5}$

38. $\frac{7}{6} - \frac{2}{3}$ or $\frac{3}{5} - \frac{5}{10}$

For Exercises 39–44, find each sum or difference.

39. $2\frac{5}{6} + 1\frac{1}{3}$

40. $15\frac{5}{8} + 10\frac{5}{6}$

41. $4\frac{4}{9} + 2\frac{1}{5}$

42. $6\frac{1}{4} - 2\frac{5}{6}$

43. $3\frac{1}{2} - 1\frac{4}{5}$

44. $8\frac{2}{3} - 6\frac{5}{7}$

For Exercises 45–50, find each sum. Describe any patterns that you see.

45. $\frac{1}{2} + \frac{1}{4}$

46. $\frac{1}{3} + \frac{1}{6}$

47. $\frac{1}{4} + \frac{1}{8}$

48. $\frac{1}{5} + \frac{1}{10}$

49. $\frac{1}{6} + \frac{1}{12}$

50. $\frac{1}{7} + \frac{1}{14}$

51. Tony works at a pizza shop. He cuts two pizzas into eight equal sections each. Customers then eat $\frac{7}{8}$ of each pizza. Tony says that $\frac{7}{8} + \frac{7}{8} = \frac{14}{16}$, so $\frac{14}{16}$ of all of the pizza was eaten. Is Tony's addition correct? Explain.

Connections

52. The rectangle shown represents 150% of a whole. Draw 100% of the same whole.

53. The beans shown represent $\frac{3}{5}$ of the total beans on the kitchen counter. How many total beans are there on the counter?

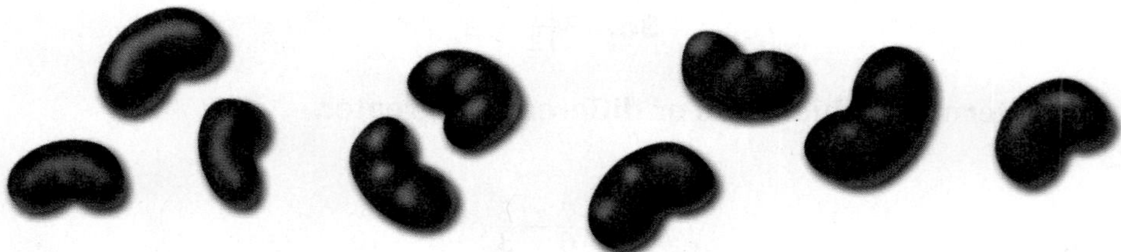

54. The following fractions occur often in our lives. It is useful to quickly recall their decimal and percent equivalents.

$\frac{1}{2}$ $\frac{1}{3}$ $\frac{1}{4}$ $\frac{2}{3}$ $\frac{3}{4}$ $\frac{1}{6}$ $\frac{1}{5}$ $\frac{1}{8}$

a. For each of these important fractions, give the decimal and percent equivalents.

b. Draw a number line. On your number line, mark the point that corresponds to each fraction shown above. Label each point with its fraction and decimal equivalent.

55. Multiple Choice Which set of decimals is ordered from least to greatest?

A. 5.603 5.63 5.096 5.67 5.599

B. 5.63 5.67 5.096 5.599 5.603

C. 5.096 5.63 5.67 5.603 5.599

D. 5.096 5.599 5.603 5.63 5.67

56. In which of the following groups of fractions can *all* of the fractions be renamed as a whole number of hundredths? Explain your reasoning for each group.

a. $\frac{3}{2}, \frac{3}{4}, \frac{3}{5}$

b. $\frac{7}{10}, \frac{7}{11}, \frac{7}{12}$

c. $\frac{2}{5}, \frac{2}{6}, \frac{2}{8}$

d. $\frac{11}{5}, \frac{11}{10}, \frac{11}{20}$

57. Suppose you select a number in the interval from $\frac{1}{2}$ to $\frac{3}{4}$ and a number in the interval from $\frac{3}{4}$ to $1\frac{1}{4}$. (Note: The numbers $\frac{1}{2}$ and $\frac{3}{4}$ are included in the interval from $\frac{1}{2}$ to $\frac{3}{4}$. The numbers $\frac{3}{4}$ and $1\frac{1}{4}$ are included in the interval from $\frac{3}{4}$ to $1\frac{1}{4}$.)

a. What is the least possible sum for these two numbers? Explain your reasoning.

b. What is the greatest possible sum for these two numbers? Explain your reasoning.

For a number sentence, the word *solve* means to find the value that makes the number sentence true. Solve Exercises 58–61.

58. $\frac{3}{12} = \frac{N}{8}$

59. $\frac{N}{4} = \frac{6}{8}$

60. $\frac{N}{12} = \frac{2}{3}$

61. $\frac{5}{12} = \frac{10}{N}$

In Exercises 62–64, paint has spilled on the page, covering part of the fraction strips. You can identify important information about each set of strips by looking at what is shown. The question marks indicate equivalent fractions of the strips. Name the equivalent fractions indicated by the question marks.

62.

63.

64.

For Exercises 65 and 66, copy each pair of numbers. Insert < , >, or = to make a true statement.

65. 18.156 ■ 18.17

66. 4.0074 ■ 4.0008

For Exercises 67 and 68, use the map of Tupelo Township.

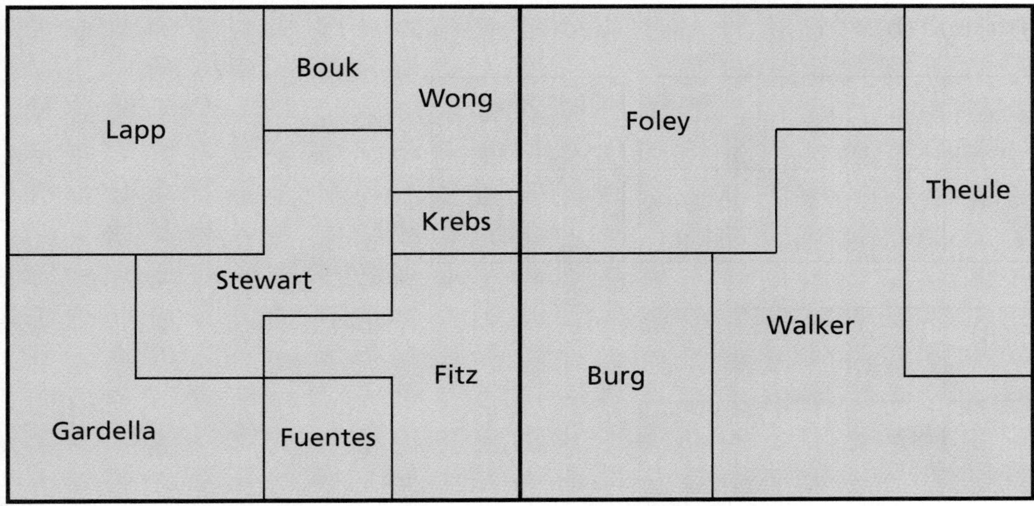

67. Multiple Choice Choose the combination of landowners who together own exactly one hundred percent of a section.

F. Burg, Lapp, Wong, Fuentes, and Bouck

G. Burg, Lapp, Fuentes, Bouck, Wong, Theule, and Stewart

H. Lapp, Fitz, Foley, and Walker

J. Walker, Foley, Fitz, and Fuentes

68. Find two different combinations of landowners whose total land is equal to 1.25 sections. Write number sentences to show your solutions.

69. The figure below represents $\frac{1}{3}$ of a whole.

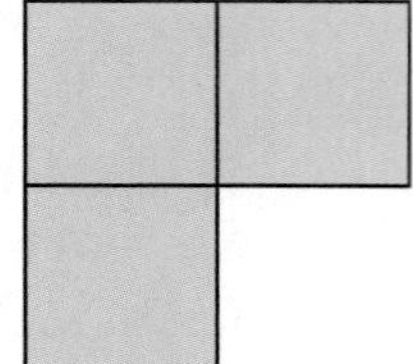

Use the figure to name the amounts shown in parts (a) and (b).

a. 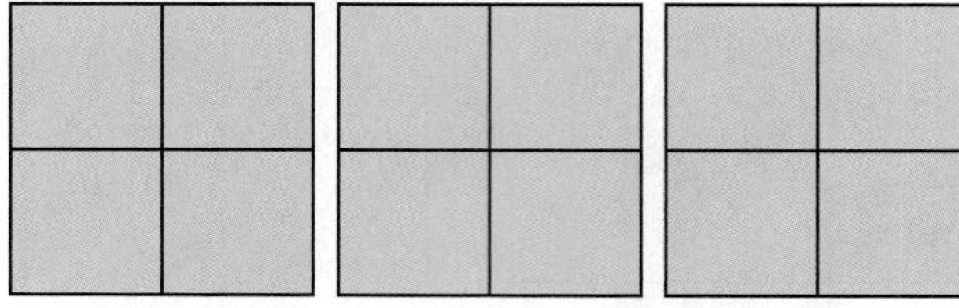

b. 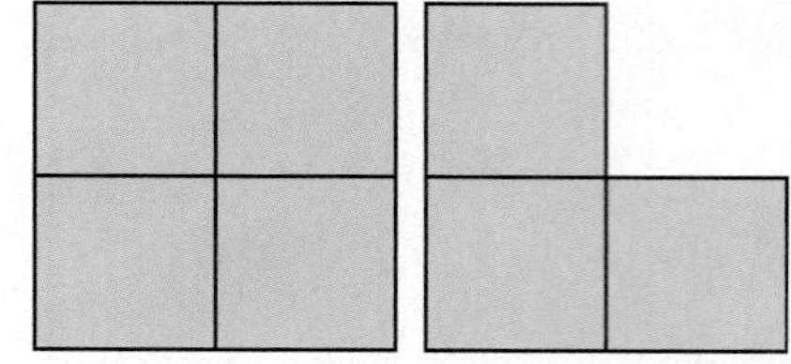

70. The following figure represents one whole.

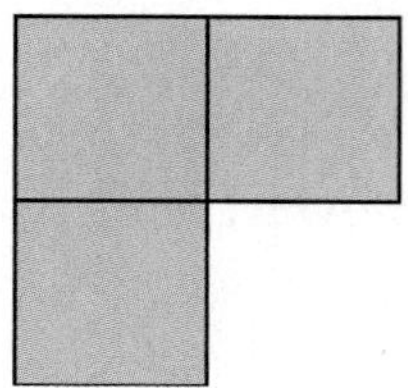

a. Draw a picture to represent $1\frac{1}{3} + \frac{1}{6}$.

b. Draw a picture to represent $2\frac{2}{3} - \frac{4}{3}$.

71. When adding $\frac{7}{15} + \frac{2}{10}$, Maribel writes $\frac{70}{150} + \frac{30}{150}$.

a. Show why $\frac{70}{150} + \frac{30}{150}$ is equivalent to $\frac{7}{15} + \frac{2}{10}$.

b. Write two more addition problems that are equivalent to $\frac{7}{15} + \frac{2}{10}$.

c. Consider the three problems, Maribel's problem and the two you wrote. Which is the easiest to use to find the sum? Why?

Extensions

For Exercises 72–74, use the number line below.

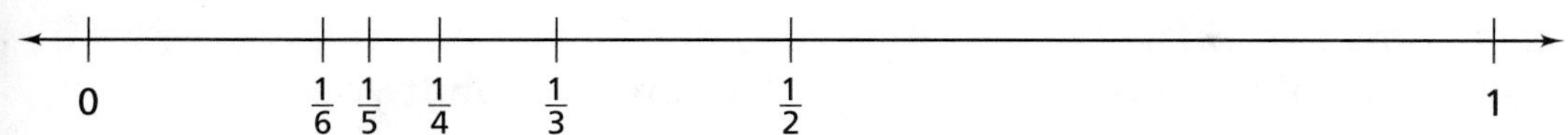

72. Name a fraction between $\frac{1}{3}$ and $\frac{1}{2}$.

73. Name a fraction between $\frac{1}{4}$ and $\frac{1}{3}$.

74. For Exercises 72 and 73, can you find another fraction in each interval? Explain.

75. *The Spartan* magazine charges $160 for each full page of advertising.

a. Identify the cost for each ad size shown below.

$\frac{1}{32}$-page, $\frac{1}{16}$-page, $\frac{1}{8}$-page, $\frac{1}{4}$-page, $\frac{1}{2}$-page, 1-page

b. Use the costs you found. What is the bill for the Cool Sub Shop if the owner purchases three $\frac{1}{4}$-page ads, four $\frac{1}{8}$-page ads, and one $\frac{1}{16}$-page ad?

c. The senior class is raising money for a trip. They have $80 to spend on advertising. Can they purchase two $\frac{1}{8}$-page ads and four $\frac{1}{16}$-page ads? Explain.

d. Find four different sets of ad sizes that the senior class can purchase for $80. Show why your answers are correct.

76. It takes 8 people to clear an acre of weeds in 4 hours.

a. How many acres can 16 people clear in 4 hours?

b. How many acres can 2 people clear in 4 hours?

c. How many people are needed to clear 3 acres in 4 hours?

d. How many people are needed to clear 3 acres in 2 hours?

77. a. Find a number for each *denominator* to make the number sentence below true. If necessary, you may use a number more than once.

$$\frac{1}{\blacksquare} - \frac{1}{\blacksquare} = \frac{1}{\blacksquare}$$

b. Find a different solution for part (a).

Mathematical Reflections 1

In this Investigation, you developed strategies for estimating the sum or difference of fractions and decimals. You then found exact sums and differences of fractions and mixed numbers. The following questions will help you summarize what you have learned.

Think about these questions. Discuss your ideas with other students and your teacher. Then write a summary of your findings in your notebook.

1. **a.** **What** are some situations in which estimating a sum or difference is useful? **Why** is estimation useful in these situations?

   b. **When** is it useful to overestimate? **When** is it useful to underestimate?

2. **When** should you use addition to solve a problem involving fractions? **When** should you use subtraction?

3. Suppose you are helping a student who has not studied fractions. **Explain** to him or her how to add and subtract fractions. Give an example of the type you think is easiest to explain. Give an example of the type you think is hardest to explain.

Common Core Mathematical Practices

As you worked on the Problems in this Investigation, you used prior knowledge to make sense of them. You also applied Mathematical Practices to solve the Problems. Think back over your work, the ways you thought about the Problems, and how you used Mathematical Practices.

Shawna described her thoughts in the following way:

For Problem 1.1, my group knew that the sum $\frac{3}{4} + \frac{4}{3}$ was closest to the benchmark number 2. We knew this because $\frac{3}{4}$ is a little less than 1, and $\frac{4}{3}$ is a little more than 1. But, we did not know if the sum was greater than 2 or less than 2.

After a while, Mia said that $\frac{4}{3}$ is $\frac{1}{3}$ of a unit away from 1. If you add $\frac{1}{3}$ to $\frac{3}{4}$, it is greater than 1. So $\frac{1}{3} + \frac{3}{4} + \frac{3}{3}$ must be greater than 2.

Common Core Standards for Mathematical Practice

MP6 Attend to precision.

- What other Mathematical Practices can you identify in Shawna's reasoning?
- Describe a Mathematical Practice that you and your classmates used to solve a different Problem in this Investigation.

Building on Multiplication With Fractions

Sometimes, instead of adding or subtracting numbers, you need to multiply them. For example, suppose you take inventory at a sporting goods store. There are thirteen full boxes and one half-full box of footballs in the storeroom. Twelve footballs fit in each full box.

- How can you find the total number of footballs without opening the boxes? Why does multiplication make sense in this situation?

In this Investigation, you will use multiplication to solve problems involving fractions. Remember, to make sense of a situation, you can draw a model or change a fraction to an equivalent form. You can also estimate to see if your answer makes sense.

2.1 How Much of the Pan Have We Sold?

Finding Parts of Parts

Paulo and Shania work at the brownie booth at the school fair. Sometimes they have to find a fractional part of another fraction. For example, a customer might ask to purchase $\frac{1}{3}$ of the brownies in a pan that is $\frac{2}{3}$ full.

- How much is $\frac{1}{3}$ of $\frac{2}{3}$?

Common Core State Standards

6.EE.A.3 Apply the properties of operations to generate equivalent expressions.

Essential for 6.NS.A.1 Interpret and compute quotients of fractions, and solve word problems involving division of fractions by fractions, e.g., by using visual fraction models and equations to represent the problem.

Problem 2.1

All of the pans of brownies are square. A pan of brownies costs \$12. You can buy any fractional part of a pan of brownies and pay that fraction of \$12. For example, $\frac{1}{2}$ of a pan costs $\frac{1}{2}$ of \$12, or \$6. We can write this as a number sentence using *of*: $\frac{1}{2}$ of $12 = 6$.

A Mr. Williams asks to buy $\frac{1}{2}$ of a pan of brownies that is $\frac{2}{3}$ full.

1. Use a copy of the brownie pan model shown at the right. Draw a picture to show how the brownie pan might look before Mr. Williams buys his brownies.
2. On the same model, use a different color to show the part of the brownies that Mr. Williams buys. Note that Mr. Williams buys a *part of a part* of the brownie pan.
3. What fraction of a whole pan of brownies does Mr. Williams buy? How much does he pay? Write number sentences using *of* to show your thinking.

Model of a Brownie Pan

B Serena buys $\frac{3}{4}$ of another pan that is half full.

1. Draw a picture to show how the brownie pan might look before Serena buys her brownies.
2. Use a different color to show the part Serena buys.
3. What fraction of a whole pan of brownies does Serena buy? How much does she pay? Write number sentences using *of* to show your thinking.

C Draw a brownie pan picture for each example below. Then write a number sentence using *of* for each. Find the part of a whole brownie pan that results.

1. $\frac{1}{3}$ of $\frac{1}{4}$ of a brownie pan
2. $\frac{1}{4}$ of $\frac{1}{3}$ of a brownie pan
3. $\frac{1}{3}$ of $\frac{3}{4}$ of a brownie pan
4. $\frac{3}{4}$ of $\frac{2}{5}$ of a brownie pan

continued on the next page >

Problem 2.1 continued

D The pictures below are models of brownie pan problems. Consider *orange* to be the portion of the brownie pan that is purchased. Consider *blue* to be the portion of the brownie pan that is left in the pan. For each picture, write a number sentence using *of* to describe what fraction of the brownie pan is purchased.

1. 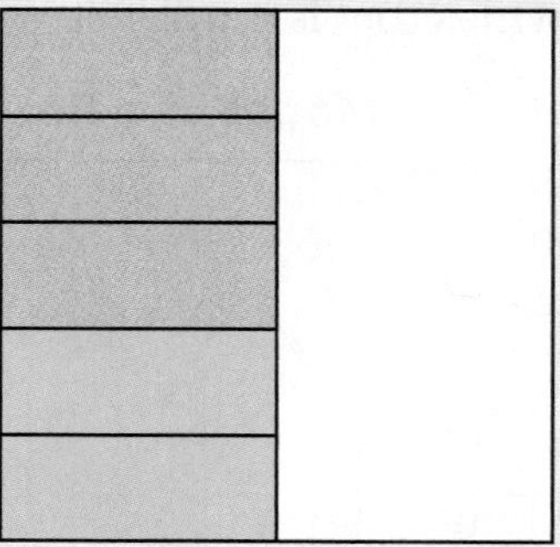

2. 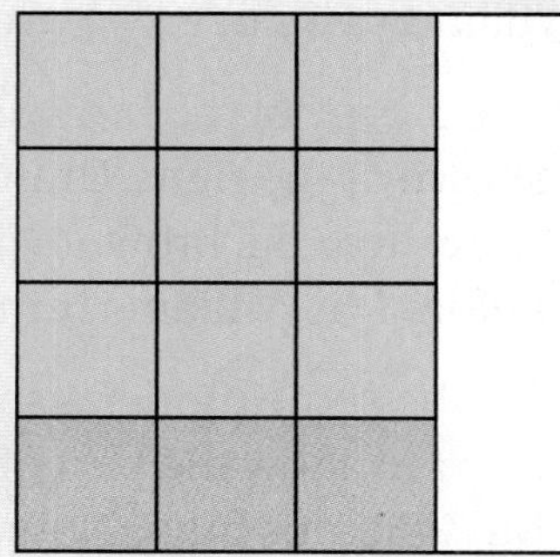

3. 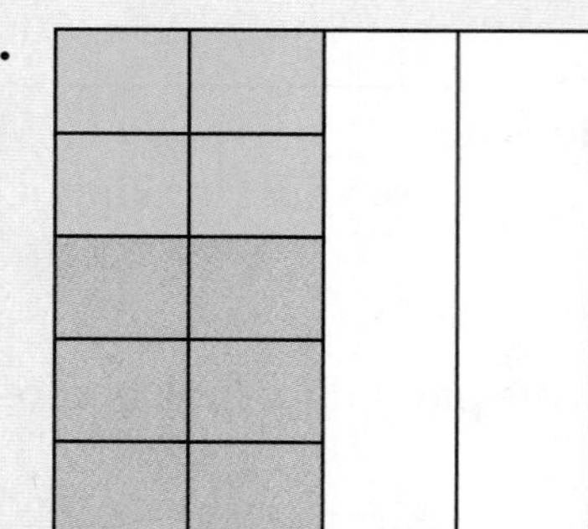

4. 

E
1. Draw pictures to check that each of the following number sentences is correct.
   a. $\frac{3}{4}$ of $\frac{1}{2} = \frac{3}{8}$
   b. $\frac{2}{5}$ of $\frac{4}{5} = \frac{8}{25}$
2. What pattern do you notice in the denominators? How does this pattern relate to your drawings?
3. What pattern do you notice in the numerators? How does this pattern relate to your drawings?
4. Paulo says that when you find a *part of a part,* your answer will always be less than either of the original parts. Is this true? Explain your reasoning.

Homework starts on page 37.

2.2 Modeling Multiplication Situations

You have used *of* in multiplication statements with whole numbers. For example:

$$2 \text{ groups } \textit{of } 12 = 2 \times 12 = 24$$

In Problem 2.1, you wrote number sentences such as:

$$\frac{3}{4} \textit{ of } \frac{1}{2} = \frac{3}{8}$$

Mathematicians use multiplication to rewrite number sentences involving fractions. When you multiply a fraction by a fraction, you are finding part of a part:

$$\frac{3}{4} \times \frac{1}{2} = \frac{3}{8}$$

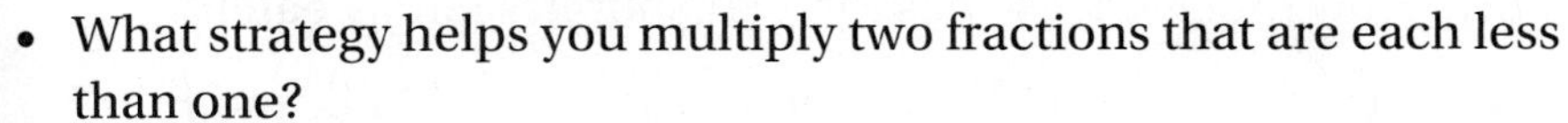

- What strategy helps you multiply two fractions that are each less than one?

You can also model multiplication situations that involve mixed numbers.

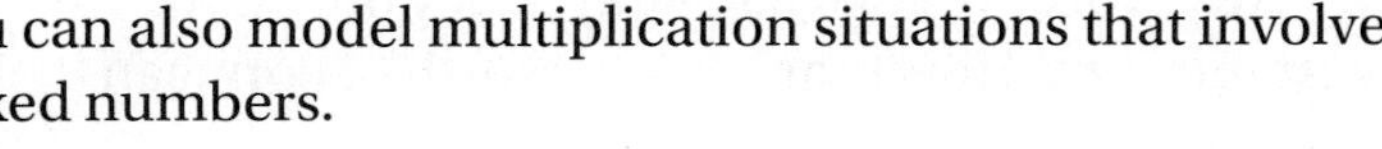

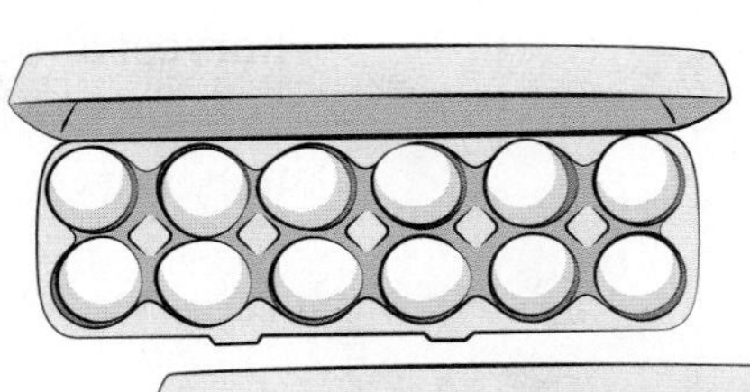

$$2\frac{1}{2} \text{ groups } \textit{of } 12 = 2 \text{ groups } \textit{of } 12 \textit{ and } \frac{1}{2} \text{ group } \textit{of } 12$$
$$= 2 \times 12 + \frac{1}{2} \times 12$$
$$= 24 + 6$$
$$= 30$$

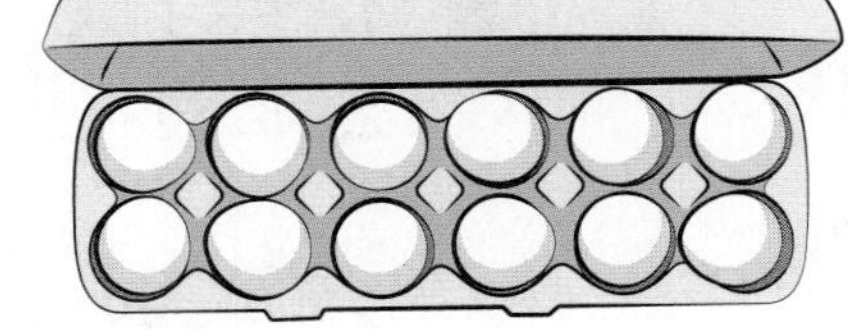

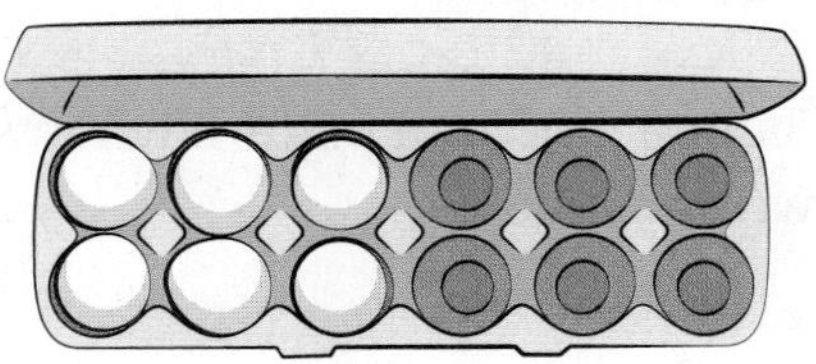

Do you think these multiplication strategies will work for all kinds of fractions?

In this Problem, you will work with multiplication situations that use fractions, whole numbers, and mixed numbers.

Problem 2.2

A For parts (1)–(3):

- Estimate the answer.
- Draw a model or a diagram to find the exact answer.
- Write a number sentence.

1. A recipe calls for $\frac{2}{3}$ of a 16-ounce bag of chocolate chips. How many ounces are needed?
2. Mr. Flansburgh buys a $2\frac{1}{2}$-pound block of cheese. His family eats $\frac{1}{3}$ of the block. How much cheese has Mr. Flansburgh's family eaten?
3. Malik and Erin run the corn harvester for Mr. Avery. Malik and Erin harvest about $2\frac{1}{3}$ acres' worth of corn each day. They only have $10\frac{1}{2}$ days to harvest the corn. How many acres' worth of corn can they harvest for Mr. Avery?

B For each number sentence below, write a story problem and find the answer.

1. $\frac{5}{6} \times 1$
2. $\frac{3}{7} \times 2$
3. $\frac{1}{2} \times \frac{9}{3}$
4. $\frac{9}{10} \times \frac{10}{7}$

C Jacinta notices a pattern when she multiplies fractions. Her pattern is written below.

> When you multiply with fractions, the product is less than each of the two factors.

Is Jacinta's pattern correct for the fractions you worked with in Questions A and B? Explain your reasoning.

D Describe a strategy for multiplying any two fractions.

ACE Homework starts on page 37.

2.3 Changing Forms

Multiplication With Mixed Numbers

You have developed some strategies for modeling multiplication and finding products of fractions. This Problem will give you a chance to formulate your strategies into algorithms. Before you begin a problem, always ask yourself:

- About how large will the product be?

Problem 2.3

A **1.** Takoda and Yuri are computing $\frac{1}{2} \times 2\frac{2}{3}$. What is a reasonable estimate for this product?

2. Takoda and Yuri each use a different strategy.

Takoda's Strategy

I used what I know about fractions to rewrite $2\frac{2}{3}$ as $\frac{8}{3}$ to make the problem easier to solve.

$$\begin{aligned}\frac{1}{2} \times 2\frac{2}{3} &= \frac{1}{2} \times \frac{8}{3}\\ &= \frac{8}{6}\\ &= 1\frac{2}{6}\\ &= 1\frac{1}{3}\end{aligned}$$

Yuri's Strategy

I wrote $2\frac{2}{3}$ as $\left(2 + \frac{2}{3}\right)$ and used the Distributive Property to make the problem easier to solve.

$$\begin{aligned}\frac{1}{2} \times 2\frac{2}{3} &= \frac{1}{2} \times \left(2 + \frac{2}{3}\right)\\ &= \left(\frac{1}{2} \times 2\right) + \left(\frac{1}{2} \times \frac{2}{3}\right)\\ &= 1 + \frac{2}{6}\\ &= 1\frac{2}{6}\\ &= 1\frac{1}{3}\end{aligned}$$

a. Does each strategy work? How do you know?

b. How are the strategies similar? How are they different?

3. Use both strategies to solve $1\frac{1}{3} \times \frac{4}{5}$. Then check your answer with a drawing.

continued on the next page >

Problem 2.3 *continued*

B For each problem below:

- Estimate the product.
- Use a multiplication strategy to find the exact product.
- Be sure to show your work.

1. $3\frac{4}{5} \times \frac{1}{4}$ **2.** $\frac{3}{4} \times 16$

3. $2\frac{1}{2} \times 1\frac{1}{6}$ **4.** $1\frac{1}{3} \times 3\frac{6}{7}$

5. $1\frac{1}{5} \times 2\frac{1}{4}$ **6.** $12 \times 4\frac{4}{9}$

C **1.** Lisa tries to use Yuri's strategy to find $4\frac{1}{2} \times 1\frac{1}{3}$. She writes:

$$4 \times 1 + \frac{1}{2} \times \frac{1}{3} = 4\frac{1}{6}$$

Yuri says that $4\frac{1}{6}$ is too small. Do you agree with Lisa or Yuri? Explain your reasoning.

2. Yuri tries to help Lisa. Yuri writes:

$$4 \times 1\frac{1}{3} + \frac{1}{2} \times 1\frac{1}{3}$$

How is this different from what Lisa wrote?

D Describe an algorithm for multiplying any two fractions, including mixed numbers.

ACE Homework starts on page 37.

Did You Know?

When you reverse the placement of the numbers in the numerator and the denominator of a fraction, a new fraction is formed. This new fraction is the **reciprocal** of the original. For example, $\frac{8}{7}$ is the reciprocal of $\frac{7}{8}$, and $\frac{12}{17}$ is the reciprocal of $\frac{17}{12}$, or $1\frac{5}{12}$. Notice that the product of a fraction and its reciprocal is 1. Why is this?

Applications

1. A pan of brownies is $\frac{7}{10}$ full. Tyreese buys $\frac{2}{5}$ of the brownies.
   a. Draw a picture of how the brownie pan looks before and after Tyreese buys his brownies.
   b. What fraction of a whole pan of brownies does Tyreese buy?

2. a. Draw brownie-pan models to show whether or not $\frac{2}{3}$ of $\frac{3}{4}$ of a pan of brownies is the same amount as $\frac{3}{4}$ of $\frac{2}{3}$ of a pan of brownies.
   b. If the brownie pans are the same size, how do the amounts of brownies from part (a) compare?
   c. Describe the relationship between $\frac{2}{3}$ of $\frac{3}{4}$ and $\frac{3}{4}$ of $\frac{2}{3}$.

3. Ms. Vargas owns $\frac{4}{5}$ of an acre of land in Tupelo Township. She wants to sell $\frac{2}{3}$ of her land to her neighbor.
   a. What fraction of an acre does Ms. Vargas want to sell? Draw a picture to illustrate your thinking.
   b. Write a number sentence that can be used to solve the problem.

4. Find each answer.
   a. $\frac{1}{2}$ of $\frac{1}{3}$
   b. $\frac{1}{2}$ of $\frac{1}{4}$
   c. $\frac{1}{2}$ of $\frac{2}{3}$
   d. $\frac{1}{2}$ of $\frac{3}{4}$
   e. Describe any patterns that you see in parts (a)–(d).

5. Answer each part without finding the exact answer. Explain your reasoning.
   a. Is $\frac{3}{4} \times 1$ greater than or less than 1?
   b. Is $\frac{3}{4} \times \frac{2}{3}$ greater than or less than 1?
   c. Is $\frac{3}{4} \times \frac{2}{3}$ greater than or less than $\frac{2}{3}$?
   d. Is $\frac{3}{4} \times \frac{2}{3}$ greater than or less than $\frac{3}{4}$?

For Exercises 6–9, write a number sentence. Use a fraction that is both positive and less than 1.

6. a fraction and a whole number with a whole number product
7. a fraction and a whole number with a product less than 1
8. a fraction and a whole number with a product greater than 1
9. a fraction and a whole number with a product between $\frac{1}{2}$ and 1

10. Shonice is making snack bags for her daughter's field hockey team. She puts $\frac{3}{4}$ cup of pretzels, $\frac{2}{3}$ cup of popcorn, $\frac{1}{3}$ cup of peanuts, and $\frac{1}{4}$ cup of chocolate chips in each bag.
    a. She wants to make 12 snack bags. How much of each ingredient does she need?
    b. Shonice decides that she would like to make snack bags for her card club. There are 15 people in the card club. How much of each ingredient will she need?

11. a. When Sierra gets home, $\frac{3}{4}$ of a sandwich is left in the refrigerator. She cuts the remaining part into three equal parts and eats two of them. What fraction of the whole sandwich did she eat?
    b. Write a number sentence to show your computation.

12. Mr. Jablonski's class is making fudge for a bake sale. Mr. Jablonski has a recipe that makes $\frac{3}{4}$ pound of fudge. There are 21 students in the class. Each student uses the recipe to make one batch of fudge. How many pounds of fudge do the students make?

13. Estimate each product. Explain your reasoning.
    a. $\frac{2}{3} \times 8\frac{5}{6}$
    b. $\frac{2}{3} \times 14\frac{1}{2}$
    c. $2\frac{1}{2} \times \frac{2}{3}$

14. Esteban is making turtle brownies. The recipe calls for $\frac{3}{4}$ bag of caramel squares. One bag has 24 caramel squares in it.
    a. How many caramel squares should Esteban use to make one batch of turtle brownies?
    b. Esteban decides to make two batches of turtle brownies. Write a number sentence to show how many bags of caramel squares he will use.

15. Isabel is adding a sun porch onto her house. She finds that covering the entire floor requires 12 rows of tiles with $11\frac{1}{3}$ tiles in each row. Write a number sentence to show how many tiles Isabel needs.

16. Judi is making a frame for a square painting. The square painting is $11\frac{3}{8}$ inches on each side.

To make sure that she has enough wood, Judi wants to buy two extra inches of wood for each corner. How much wood should Judi buy?

17. Find each product.

a. $\frac{1}{3} \times 18$

b. $\frac{2}{3} \times 18$

c. $\frac{5}{3} \times 18$

d. $1\frac{2}{3} \times 18$

e. What patterns do you see in these products?

18. Carolyn is making cookies. The recipe calls for $1\frac{3}{4}$ cups of brown sugar. If she makes $2\frac{1}{2}$ batches of cookies, how much brown sugar does she need?

For Exercises 19–27, use an algorithm for multiplying fractions to determine each product.

19. $\frac{5}{12} \times 1\frac{1}{3}$

20. $\frac{2}{7} \times \frac{7}{8}$

21. $3\frac{2}{9} \times \frac{7}{3}$

22. $2\frac{2}{5} \times 1\frac{1}{15}$

23. $10\frac{3}{4} \times 2\frac{2}{3}$

24. $1\frac{1}{8} \times \frac{4}{7}$

25. $\frac{11}{6} \times \frac{9}{10}$

26. $\frac{9}{4} \times 1\frac{1}{6}$

27. $\frac{5}{2} \times \frac{8}{11}$

Connections

28. Bianca and Yoko work together to mow the lawn. Suppose Yoko mows $\frac{5}{12}$ of the lawn and Bianca mows $\frac{2}{5}$ of the lawn. How much lawn still needs to be mowed?

29. Joe and Ashanti need $2\frac{2}{5}$ bushels of apples to make applesauce. Suppose Joe picks $1\frac{5}{6}$ bushels of apples. How many more bushels need to be picked?

30. Roshaun and Lea go to an amusement park. Lea spends $\frac{1}{2}$ of her money, and Roshaun spends $\frac{1}{4}$ of his money. Is it possible for Roshaun to have spent more money than Lea? Explain your reasoning.

31. Min Ji uses balsa wood to build airplane models.

After completing a model, she has a strip of balsa wood measuring $\frac{7}{8}$ yard left over. Shawn wants to buy half of the strip from Min Ji. How long is the strip of wood Shawn wants to buy?

32. Aran has a bag of pretzels for a snack. He gives half of the pretzels to Jon. Then, Jon gives Kiona $\frac{1}{3}$ of his portion. What fraction of the bag of pretzels does each person get?

33. Mr. Mace's class is planning a field trip, and $\frac{3}{5}$ of his students want to go to Chicago. Of those who want to go to Chicago, $\frac{2}{3}$ want to go to Navy Pier. What fraction of the class wants to go to Navy Pier?

34. In Vashon's class, three fourths of the students are girls. Four fifths of the girls in the class have brown hair.

a. What fraction represents the girls in Vashon's class with brown hair?

b. How many students are in Vashon's class? Explain your reasoning.

35. Violeta and Mandy are making beaded necklaces. They have beads of various colors and sizes. As they design patterns, they want to find out how long the final necklace will be. They have the following bead widths to work with:

Widths of Beads

Bead	Width
Small Trade Neck	$\frac{1}{4}$ inch
Medium Trade Neck	$\frac{3}{8}$ inch
Large Trade Neck	$\frac{7}{16}$ inch

a. Mandy makes the necklace below. She uses 30 small Trade Neck beads, 6 medium Trade Neck beads, and 1 large Trade Neck bead. How long is Mandy's necklace?

b. Violeta wants to make a 16-inch necklace by alternating medium and large Trade Neck beads. She only has 8 medium Trade Neck beads. If she uses 8 medium Trade Neck beads and 8 large Trade Neck beads, will her necklace be 16 inches long?

36. Multiple Choice Which of the numbers below, when multiplied by $\frac{4}{7}$, will be greater than $\frac{4}{7}$?

A. $\frac{1}{7}$ **B.** $\frac{7}{7}$ **C.** $\frac{17}{7}$ **D.** $\frac{4}{7}$

37. Multiple Choice Which of the numbers below, when multiplied by $\frac{4}{7}$, will be less than $\frac{4}{7}$?

F. $\frac{1}{7}$ **G.** $\frac{7}{7}$ **H.** $\frac{17}{7}$ **J.** $\frac{8}{7}$

38. Multiple Choice Which of the numbers below, when multiplied by $\frac{4}{7}$, will be exactly $\frac{4}{7}$?

A. $\frac{1}{7}$ **B.** $\frac{7}{7}$ **C.** $\frac{17}{7}$ **D.** $\frac{4}{7}$

For Exercises 39–42, find each product.

39. $\frac{1}{3}$ of $\frac{2}{3}$

40. $\frac{5}{6}$ of 3

41. $\frac{2}{3}$ of $\frac{5}{6}$

42. $\frac{2}{5}$ of $\frac{5}{8}$

43. **a.** How many minutes are in 1 hour?

b. How many minutes are in $\frac{1}{2}$ hour?

c. How many minutes are in 0.5 hour?

d. How many minutes are in 0.1 hour?

e. How many minutes are in 1.25 hours?

f. How many hours are in 186 minutes? Express this as a mixed number and as a decimal.

44. Terry wants to make $\frac{1}{2}$ of a batch of chocolate chip cookies. Rewrite her recipe so that she only needs $\frac{1}{2}$ as much of each ingredient.

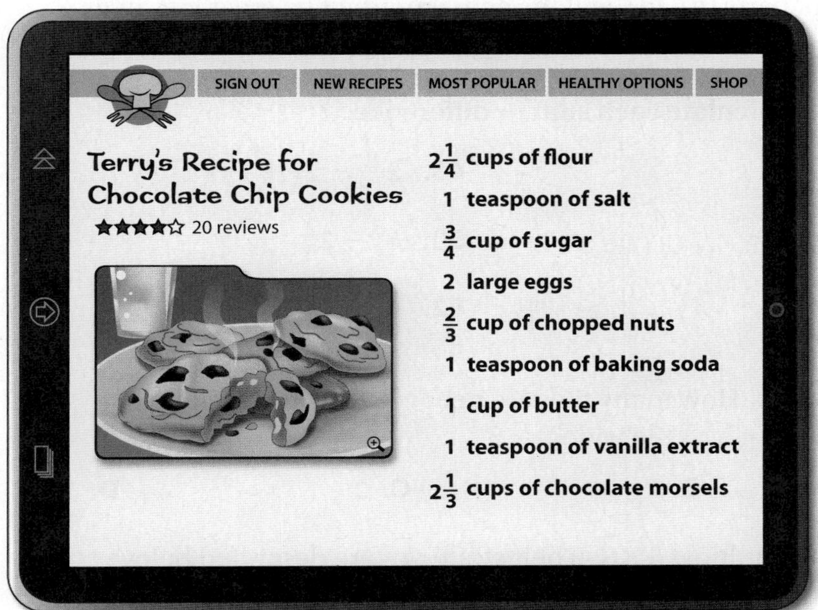

SIGN OUT
NEW RECIPES
MOST POPULAR
HEALTHY OPTIONS
SHOP
Terry's Recipe for Chocolate Chip Cookies
20 reviews
$2\frac{1}{4}$ cups of flour
1 teaspoon of salt
$\frac{3}{4}$ cup of sugar
2 large eggs
$\frac{2}{3}$ cup of chopped nuts
1 teaspoon of baking soda
1 cup of butter
1 teaspoon of vanilla extract
$2\frac{1}{3}$ cups of chocolate morsels

45. Terry finds a recipe for chewy brownie cookies.

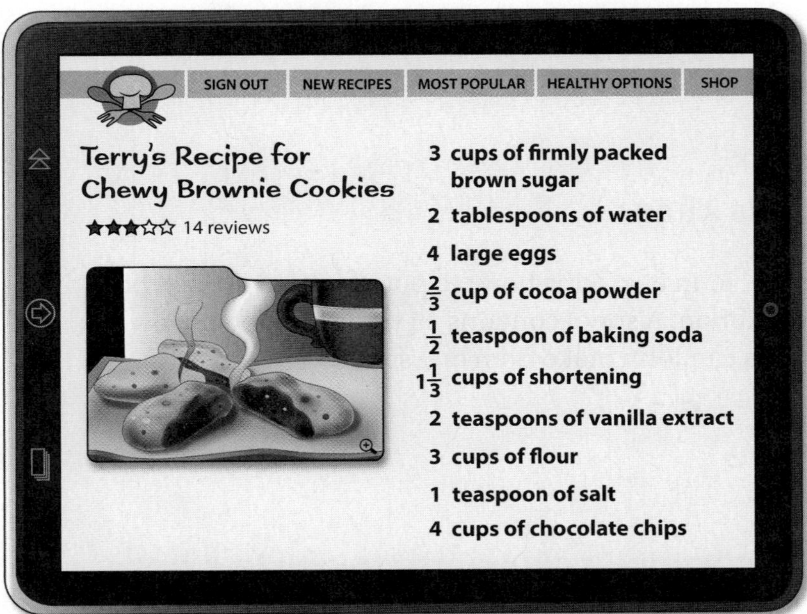

SIGN OUT
NEW RECIPES
MOST POPULAR
HEALTHY OPTIONS
SHOP
Terry's Recipe for Chewy Brownie Cookies
14 reviews
3 cups of firmly packed brown sugar
2 tablespoons of water
4 large eggs
$\frac{2}{3}$ cup of cocoa powder
$\frac{1}{2}$ teaspoon of baking soda
$1\frac{1}{3}$ cups of shortening
2 teaspoons of vanilla extract
3 cups of flour
1 teaspoon of salt
4 cups of chocolate chips

She wants to bake only $\frac{1}{4}$ of the number of cookies the recipe will make. Rewrite her recipe so that it will make $\frac{1}{4}$ as many chewy brownie cookies.

46. Estimate each product to the nearest whole number (1, 2, 3, . . .).

a. $\frac{1}{2} \times 2\frac{9}{10}$ **b.** $1\frac{1}{2} \times 2\frac{9}{10}$ **c.** $2\frac{1}{2} \times \frac{4}{7}$ **d.** $3\frac{1}{4} \times 2\frac{11}{12}$

e. For each of parts (a)–(d), will the actual product be greater than or less than your whole-number estimate? Explain.

For Exercises 47–52, calculate each sum or difference.

47. $2\frac{2}{3} + 3\frac{5}{6}$

48. $2\frac{8}{10} + 2\frac{4}{5} + 1\frac{1}{2}$

49. $4\frac{3}{10} + 2\frac{2}{6}$

50. $5\frac{5}{8} - 2\frac{2}{3}$

51. $6\frac{7}{10} - 3\frac{4}{5}$

52. $8 - 3\frac{14}{15}$

53. Multiple Choice How many tiles are needed to make a rectangle that is $4\frac{1}{3}$ tiles long by $\frac{1}{2}$ tile wide?

A. $2\frac{1}{3}$ **B.** $2\frac{1}{6}$ **C.** 2 **D.** $2\frac{1}{4}$

54. Three students multiply $6 \times \frac{1}{5}$. Their strategies are described below. The students' answers are $\frac{6}{5}$, 1.2, and $1\frac{1}{5}$. Match each answer to the strategy that is most likely to produce it. Explain your reasoning.

a. Fala draws six shapes, each representing $\frac{1}{5}$, and fits them together.

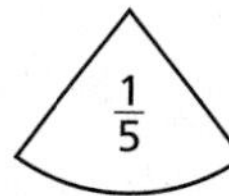

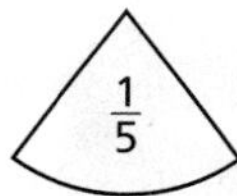

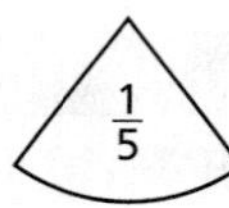

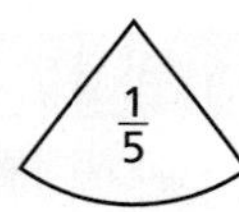

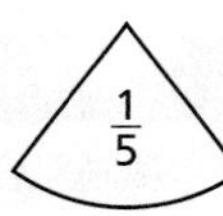

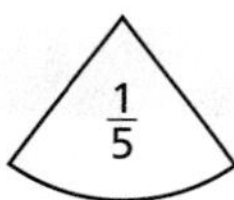

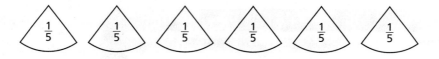

b. Jorell writes $\frac{6}{1} \times \frac{1}{5}$.

c. Hiroshi writes 6×0.2.

55. Multiple Choice John is making bows to put on wreaths. Each bow uses $2\frac{1}{3}$ yards of ribbon. A spool contains 15 yards of ribbon. How many whole bows can John make from one spool?

F. 6 **G.** 7 **H.** 12 **J.** 35

Extensions

For Exercises 56 and 57, find each product.

56. $\frac{2}{3} \times \frac{1}{2} \times \frac{3}{4}$

57. $\frac{5}{8} \times \frac{1}{2} \times \frac{2}{3}$

Mathematical Reflections 2

In this Investigation, you explored situations that required you to multiply fractions. You also developed an algorithm for multiplying fractions. The following questions will help you summarize what you have learned.

Think about these questions. Discuss your ideas with other students and your teacher. Then write a summary of your findings in your notebook.

1. **Explain** and **illustrate** what *of* means when you find a fraction *of* another number. What operation do you use when you find parts of parts?
2. **a.** If you forget the algorithm for multiplying fractions, **how** might you use rectangular models to help you multiply fractions?

   b. **Describe** an algorithm for multiplying any two fractions.

   c. **Describe** when it might be useful to estimate a product.
3. Use examples to **explain** the following statement:

   When you multiply a fraction by another fraction, your answer might be less than both factors, more than one of the factors, or more than both factors.

Common Core Mathematical Practices

As you worked on the Problems in this Investigation, you used prior knowledge to make sense of them. You also applied Mathematical Practices to solve the Problems. Think back over your work, the ways you thought about the Problems, and how you used Mathematical Practices.

Nick described his thoughts in the following way:

In Problem 2.1, we used a square brownie pan model to show what $\frac{3}{4}$ of $\frac{1}{2}$ looks like. We used the picture to find how much $\frac{3}{4}$ of $\frac{1}{2}$ is. We wrote the number sentence '$\frac{3}{4}$ of $\frac{1}{2} = \frac{3}{8}$' to represent the amount of brownies that we were finding.

This is called an area model for multiplication. The length marked along one side of the pan stands for one fraction. The length along a perpendicular side stands for the second fraction being multiplied. The answer is the area of overlap inside the pan.

Common Core Standards for Mathematical Practice
MP4 Model with mathematics.

- What other Mathematical Practices can you identify in Nick's reasoning?
- Describe a Mathematical Practice that you and your classmates used to solve a different Problem in this Investigation.

Dividing With Fractions

So far in *Let's Be Rational,* you have solved problems using addition, subtraction, and multiplication. In Investigation 3, you will solve problems that require division of fractions. As you work on these problems, think about similarities and differences among the problems.

In the number sentence $21 \div 7 = 3$, 21 is the *dividend,* 7 is the *divisor,* and 3 is the result, or *quotient.*

You can use the vocabulary of division problems as placeholders in a division number sentence. The division sentence below shows how these quantities relate to one another.

$$\text{dividend} \div \text{divisor} = \text{quotient}$$

First, you need to understand what division of fractions means. Then you can calculate quotients when the divisor or the dividend, or both, is a fraction.

Common Core State Standards

6.NS.A.1 Apply and extend previous understandings of multiplication and division to divide fractions by fractions.

6.EE.A.2b Identify parts of an expression using mathematical terms (sum, term, product, factor, quotient, coefficient); view one or more parts of an expression as a single entity.

When you do the division $12 \div 5$, what does the answer mean?

The answer should tell you how many fives are in 12 wholes. Because a whole number of fives will not fit into 12, you might write

$$12 \div 5 = 2\tfrac{2}{5}$$

Then, what does the fractional part of the answer mean?

The answer means you can make 2 fives and $\frac{2}{5}$ of *another* five.

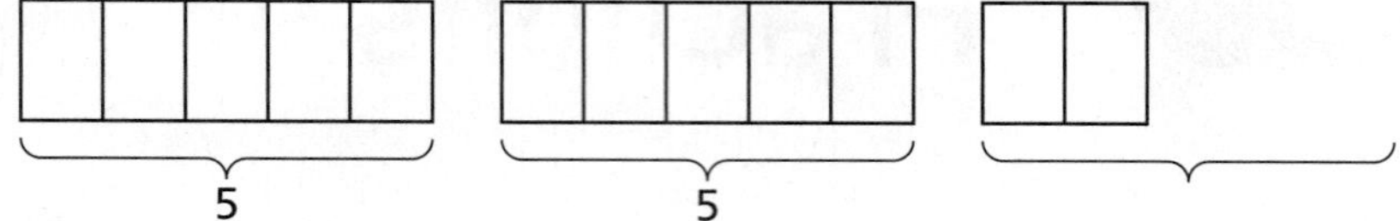

You can check your work by seeing that the related number sentence is true.

$$5 \times 2\tfrac{2}{5} = 12$$

In the division problem above, the divisor and dividend are both whole numbers. In Problem 3.1, you will explore division problems in which the divisor and dividend are both fractions. You will answer questions such as the following.

- How many $\frac{1}{4}$'s are in $\frac{1}{2}$?
- How can you draw a model to show this?
- How can you write this as a division number sentence?
- What does the answer to this division problem mean?
- What does it mean to divide a fraction by a fraction?

3.1 Preparing Food
Dividing a Fraction by a Fraction

At Humboldt Middle School football games, the students and teachers run a concession stand to raise money. Mrs. Drake's class is hosting a cookout. The students sell hamburgers to raise money.

Problem 3.1

For each question, do the following.

- Solve the problem.
- Draw a model to help explain your reasoning.
- Write a number sentence showing your calculations.
- Explain what your answer means.

A Mrs. Drake is grilling the hamburgers. Some people like big patties, some medium patties, and some small patties.

1. How many $\frac{1}{8}$-pound patties can she make from $\frac{7}{8}$ of a pound of hamburger?
2. How many $\frac{2}{8}$-pound patties can she make from $\frac{7}{8}$ of a pound of hamburger?
3. A teacher brings $2\frac{3}{4}$ pounds of hamburger to make $\frac{1}{4}$-pound patties. How many patties can he make?

B

1. Sam has $\frac{3}{4}$ of a can of hot chocolate mix for drinks to keep everyone warm. To make a cup of hot chocolate, Sam adds hot water to one scoop of hot chocolate mix. The scoop holds $\frac{1}{24}$ of a can. How many cups of hot chocolate can Sam make?
2. Tom decided not to use the $\frac{1}{24}$ scoop used by Sam. Instead, he uses a scoop that is $\frac{1}{8}$ of a can of hot chocoloate mix. Tom and Sam each start with the same amount, $\frac{3}{4}$ of a can of hot chocolate mix. Who can make more cups of hot chocolate? Explain.

C Describe a strategy for dividing a fraction by a fraction.

ACE Homework starts on page 55.

3.2 Into Pieces

Whole Numbers or Mixed Numbers Divided by Fractions

Suppose you ask, “How many $\frac{3}{4}$’s are in 14?” You can write this question as a division expression, $14 \div \frac{3}{4}$. Then you can represent it on a number line. Sam starts to use the number line below, but does not know what to do next. What should Sam do?

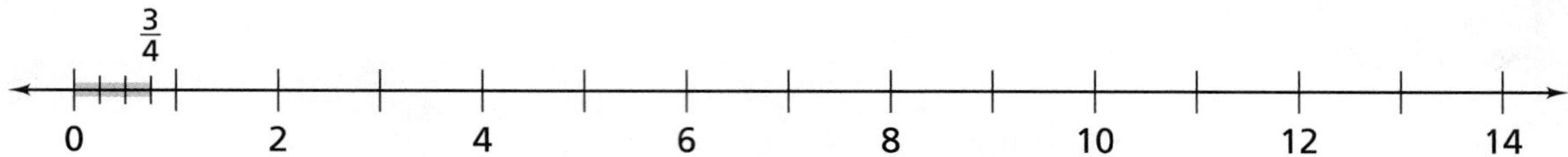

- Can you make a whole number of $\frac{3}{4}$’s out of 14 wholes? If not, what does the fractional part of the answer mean?
- What does it mean to divide a whole number or mixed number by a fraction?

Problem 3.2

For each part of Question A below, do the following.

- Solve the problem.
- Draw a model to help explain your reasoning.
- Write a number sentence that shows your reasoning.

A **1.** Naylah plans to make small cheese pizzas to sell at the school carnival. She has nine blocks of cheese. How many pizzas can she make if each pizza needs the given amount of cheese?

a. $\frac{1}{3}$ block **b.** $\frac{1}{4}$ block

c. $\frac{1}{5}$ block **d.** $\frac{2}{3}$ block

e. $\frac{3}{3}$ block **f.** $\frac{4}{3}$ block

2. The answer to part (d) above is a mixed number. What does the fractional part of the answer mean?

continued on the next page >

Problem 3.2 continued

B Use your ideas from Question A to write questions that the following expressions could fit. Then do the calculations. Be sure to label your answers.

1. $12 \div \frac{2}{3}$
2. $12 \div \frac{5}{6}$
3. $12 \div \frac{7}{6}$
4. $12 \div 1\frac{1}{3}$

C

1. Jasmine has $5\frac{1}{4}$ cups of frosting. She wants to put $\frac{3}{8}$ cup of frosting on each cupcake she makes. About how many cupcakes can she frost?
2. Chris needs $3\frac{1}{2}$ cups of flour. His only clean measuring cup holds $\frac{1}{3}$ cup. How many $\frac{1}{3}$ cups of flour does Chris need?

D Describe a strategy for dividing a whole number or a mixed number by a fraction.

ACE Homework starts on page 55.

3.3 Sharing a Prize

Dividing a Fraction by a Whole Number

At a recent school carnival, teams of students competed in contests. The members of each winning team shared prizes donated by store owners. Sharing the prizes leads to a new kind of division.

- What does it mean to divide a fraction by a whole number?

Problem 3.3

A Ms. Li gave peanuts as a prize for a relay race. The members of the winning team share the peanuts equally among themselves. What fraction of a pound of peanuts does each team member get in each situation? Use diagrams and number sentences to explain your reasoning.

1. Four students share $\frac{1}{2}$ pound of peanuts.
2. Three students share $\frac{1}{4}$ pound of peanuts.
3. Two students share $\frac{3}{4}$ pound of peanuts.
4. Four students share $1\frac{1}{2}$ pounds of peanuts.

B Find each quotient and explain how you thought about it.

1. $\frac{2}{3} \div 5$
2. $\frac{3}{2} \div 2$
3. $\frac{2}{5} \div 3$
4. $\frac{4}{5} \div 4$

C Write a story problem that can be represented by $\frac{8}{3} \div 4$. Explain why the division makes sense.

D Describe a strategy for dividing a fraction by a whole number.

ACE Homework starts on page 55.

3.4 Examining Algorithms for Dividing Fractions

In Problems 3.1, 3.2, and 3.3, you solved a variety of division problems. In Problem 3.4, you will develop an algorithm to handle all of them. You begin by dividing division problems into categories.

What is an algorithm you can use to divide any two fractions, including mixed numbers?

Problem 3.4

A For each division expression below, do the following.

- Estimate the quotient.
- Calculate the exact value of the quotient.
- State what the answer to the division expression means.

1. $\frac{1}{3} \div 9$	**2.** $12 \div \frac{1}{6}$	**3.** $\frac{5}{6} \div \frac{1}{12}$
4. $5 \div 1\frac{1}{2}$	**5.** $\frac{1}{2} \div 3\frac{2}{3}$	**6.** $\frac{3}{4} \div \frac{3}{4}$
7. $5 \div \frac{2}{3}$	**8.** $\frac{1}{6} \div 12$	**9.** $3 \div \frac{2}{5}$
10. $3\frac{1}{3} \div \frac{2}{3}$	**11.** $5\frac{2}{3} \div 1\frac{1}{2}$	**12.** $\frac{9}{5} \div \frac{1}{2}$

continued on the next page >

Problem 3.4 continued

B **1.** Sort the expressions from Question A into two groups:

- Group 1. Problems that require little work to evaluate.
- Group 2. Problems that require much work to evaluate.

2. Explain why you put each expression into the group you chose.

C Write two new division expressions involving fractions for each of your groups. Explain why each expression goes with one group.

D Write an algorithm for division involving *any* two fractions, including mixed numbers.

E Use your division algorithm to divide.

1. $9 \div \frac{4}{5}$

2. $1\frac{7}{8} \div 3$

3. $1\frac{2}{3} \div \frac{1}{5}$

4. $2\frac{5}{6} \div 1\frac{1}{3}$

F April notices that sometimes a quotient is less than one and sometimes a quotient is greater than one. What is the relationship between the dividend and the divisor in each case?

dividend ÷ divisor = quotient

ACE Homework starts on page 55.

Applications

1. A latte (LAH tay) is the most popular drink at Antonio's Coffee Shop.

Antonio makes only one size of latte, and he uses $\frac{1}{3}$ cup of milk in each drink. How many lattes can Antonio make with the amount of milk in containers (a)–(c)? If there is a remainder, what does it mean?

a. $\frac{7}{9}$ cup **b.** $\frac{5}{6}$ cup **c.** $3\frac{2}{3}$ cups

2. Write a story problem that can be solved using $1\frac{3}{4} \div \frac{1}{2}$. Explain how the calculation matches your story.

3. The Easy Baking Company makes muffins. They make several sizes, ranging from very small to very large. There are 20 cups of flour in the packages of flour they buy. How many muffins can they make from a package of flour if each muffin takes one of the following amounts of flour?

a. $\frac{1}{4}$ cup **b.** $\frac{2}{4}$ cup **c.** $\frac{3}{4}$ cup

d. $\frac{1}{10}$ cup **e.** $\frac{2}{10}$ cup **f.** $\frac{7}{10}$ cup

g. $\frac{1}{7}$ cup **h.** $\frac{2}{7}$ cup **i.** $\frac{6}{7}$ cup

j. Explain how the answers for $20 \div \frac{1}{7}$, $20 \div \frac{2}{7}$, and $20 \div \frac{6}{7}$ are related. Show why this makes sense.

For Exercises 4–7, find each quotient.

4. $6 \div \frac{3}{5}$

5. $5 \div \frac{2}{9}$

6. $3 \div \frac{1}{4}$

7. $4 \div \frac{5}{8}$

For Exercises 8–10, find each quotient. Describe any patterns that you see.

8. $5 \div \frac{1}{4}$

9. $5 \div \frac{1}{8}$

10. $5 \div \frac{1}{16}$

For Exercises 11–13, answer the question. Then draw a picture or write a number sentence to show why your answer is correct. If there is a remainder, tell what it means for the given situation.

11. Bill wants to make 22 small pizzas for a party. He has 16 cups of flour. Each pizza crust takes $\frac{3}{4}$ cup of flour. Does he have enough flour?

12. It takes $18\frac{3}{8}$ inches of wood to make a frame for a small photo. Ms. Jones has 3 yards of wood. How many frames can she make?

13. There are 12 rabbits at a pet store. The manager lets Gabriella feed vegetables to the rabbits. She has $5\frac{1}{4}$ ounces of parsley today. She wants to give each rabbit the same amount. How much parsley does each rabbit get?

14. Anoki is in charge of giving prizes to teams at a mathematics competition. With each prize, he also wants to give all the members of the team equal amounts of mints. How much will each team member get if Anoki has the given amounts of mints?

a. $\frac{1}{2}$ pound of mints for 8 students

b. $\frac{1}{4}$ pound of mints for 4 students

c. $\frac{3}{4}$ pound of mints for 3 students

d. $\frac{4}{5}$ pound of mints for 10 students

e. $1\frac{1}{2}$ pounds of mints for 2 students

15. Maria uses $5\frac{1}{3}$ gallons of gas to drive to work and back four times.

a. How many gallons of gas does Maria use in one round trip to work?

b. Maria's car gets 28 miles to the gallon. How many miles is her round trip to work?

16. **Multiple Choice** Nana's recipe for applesauce makes $8\frac{1}{2}$ cups. She serves the applesauce equally among her three grandchildren. How many cups of applesauce will each one get?

A. $\frac{3}{2}$ cups

B. $25\frac{1}{2}$ cups

C. $\frac{9}{6}$ cups

D. none of these

For Exercises 17–19, find each quotient. Draw a picture to prove that each quotient makes sense.

17. $\frac{4}{5} \div 3$

18. $1\frac{2}{3} \div 5$

19. $\frac{5}{3} \div 5$

20. Multiple Choice Which of the following diagrams represents $\frac{1}{3} \div 4$?

A. 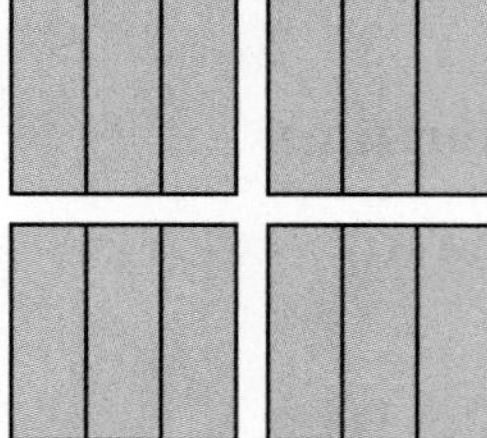

B. 

C. 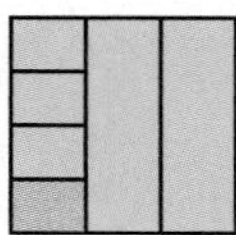

D. 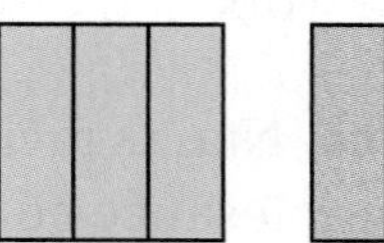

21. Multiple Choice Which of the following diagrams represents $4 \div \frac{1}{3}$?

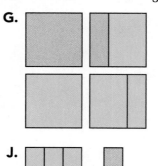

F. 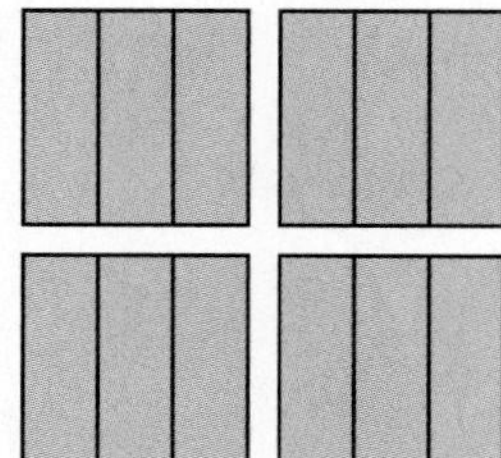

G. 

H. 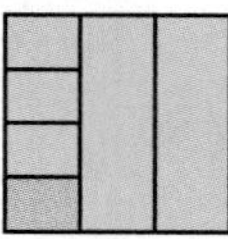

J. 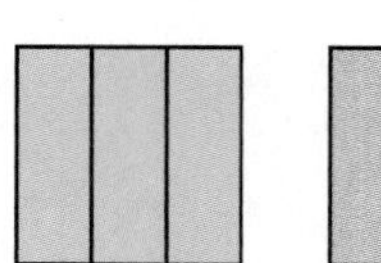

For Exercises 22–25, is each quotient greater than or less than one? Explain your reasoning.

22. $\frac{7}{9} \div \frac{1}{9}$

23. $\frac{2}{3} \div \frac{1}{9}$

24. $\frac{1}{18} \div \frac{1}{9}$

25. $1 \div \frac{1}{9}$

For Exercises 26–34, find the quotient.

26. $\frac{5}{6} \div \frac{1}{3}$

27. $\frac{2}{3} \div \frac{1}{9}$

28. $1\frac{1}{2} \div \frac{3}{8}$

29. $10 \div \frac{2}{3}$

30. $5 \div \frac{3}{4}$

31. $\frac{6}{7} \div 4$

32. $\frac{3}{10} \div 2$

33. $\frac{2}{5} \div \frac{1}{3}$

34. $2\frac{1}{2} \div 1\frac{1}{3}$

35. For Exercises 29 and 31 above, write a story problem to fit the computation.

Connections

For Exercises 36–39, find two equivalent fractions. (For example, $\frac{12}{15}$ and $\frac{24}{30}$ are equivalent fractions.) One fraction should have a numerator greater than the one given. The other fraction should have a numerator less than the one given.

36. $\frac{4}{6}$

37. $\frac{10}{12}$

38. $\frac{12}{9}$

39. $\frac{8}{6}$

40. Toshi has to work at the car wash for 3 hours. So far, he has worked $1\frac{3}{4}$ hours. How many more hours will it be before he can leave work?

For Exercises 41–44, find each sum or difference.

41. $\frac{9}{10} + \frac{1}{5}$

42. $\frac{5}{6} + \frac{7}{8}$

43. $\frac{2}{3} + 1\frac{1}{3}$

44. $12\frac{5}{6} - 8\frac{1}{4}$

For Exercises 45–48, find each product.

45. $\frac{2}{7} \times \frac{1}{3}$

46. $\frac{3}{4} \times \frac{7}{8}$

47. $1\frac{1}{2} \times \frac{1}{3}$

48. $4\frac{2}{3} \times 2\frac{3}{4}$

49. Kendra jogs $2\frac{2}{5}$ km on a trail and then sits down to wait for Louis. Louis has jogged $1\frac{1}{2}$ km on the same trail.

How much farther will Louis have to jog to reach Kendra?

50. The marks on each number line are spaced so that the distance between any two consecutive tick marks is the same. Copy each number line and label the marks.

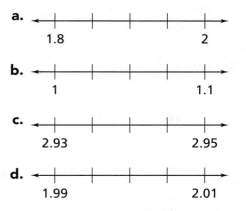

a.

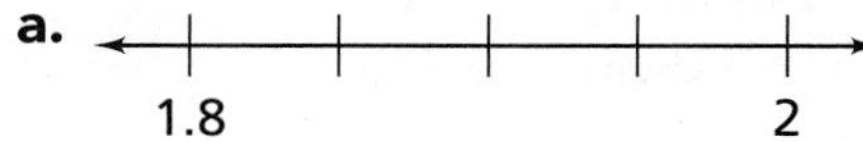

b.

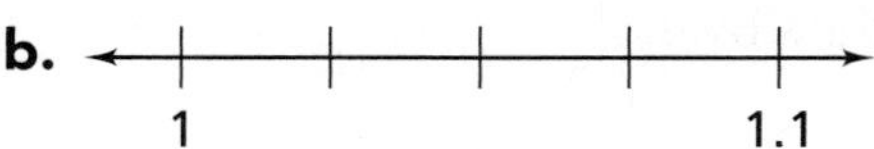

c.

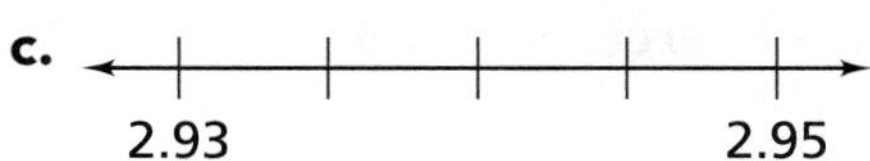

d.

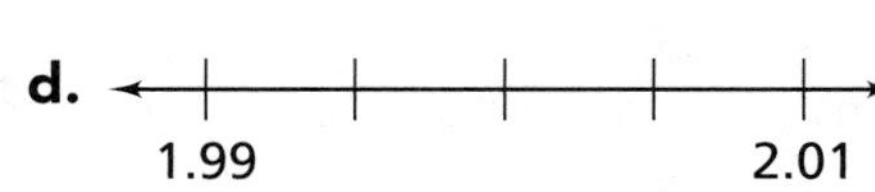

e. Explain how you determined what the labels should be.

Use the cartoon below to answer Exercises 51–53.

51. How many slices of the pizza will have olives?

52. How many slices of the pizza will be plain?

53. What fraction of the pizza will have onions and green peppers?

Extensions

54. Dante says there is an easy way to find out how many quarters are in some whole number of dollars. He says you should divide the number of dollars by $\frac{1}{4}$. Vanna says she knows an easier way. You just need to multiply the number of dollars by 4. With whom do you agree? Explain.

Use the table of equivalent measures below to solve Exercises 55–59.

Measurement	Equivalent Measurement
1 cup	16 tablespoons
1 quart	4 cups
1 quart	2 pints
1 gallon	4 quarts
1 tablespoon	3 teaspoons

55. Brian is missing his measuring cup. He needs to measure out $\frac{1}{2}$ cup of vegetable oil. How many tablespoons should he use?

56. To measure out $\frac{1}{2}$ cup of vegetable oil, how many teaspoons does Brian need?

57. What fraction of a quart is $\frac{1}{2}$ cup?

58. What fraction of a gallon is $\frac{1}{2}$ cup?

59. Suppose you need to measure out exactly one gallon of water. The only measuring scoops you have are $\frac{1}{2}$ cup, 1 cup, and 1 pint. Which scoop would you use? How would you make sure you had exactly one gallon?

Mathematical Reflections 3

In this Investigation, you developed strategies for dividing when fractions are involved. You developed algorithms to use for division problems involving fractions or mixed numbers. The following questions will help you summarize what you have learned.

Think about these questions. Discuss your ideas with other students and your teacher. Then write a summary of your findings in your notebook.

1. When solving a problem, **how** do you recognize when division is the operation you need to use?
2. a. **How** is dividing a whole number by a fraction similar to or different from dividing a fraction by a whole number?

   b. **Explain** your strategy for dividing one fraction by another fraction. Does your strategy also work for divisions where the dividend or divisor is a whole number or a mixed number? Explain.
3. When dividing a whole number by a whole number greater than 1, the quotient is always less than the dividend. For example, $15 \div 3 = 5$, and 5 is less than 15 (the dividend). Use examples to help **explain** the following statement:

   When you divide a fraction by another fraction, your answer might be greater than the dividend or less than the dividend.

Common Core Mathematical Practices

As you worked on the Problems in this Investigation, you used prior knowledge to make sense of them. You also applied Mathematical Practices to solve the Problems. Think back over your work, the ways you thought about the Problems, and how you used Mathematical Practices.

Hector described his thoughts in the following way:

In Problem 3.4, we solved and sorted all sorts of division problems. Then, we found an algorithm that works for all of them. If you make a mixed number into an improper fraction, you can use the same division algorithm all of the time.

We came up with two algorithms. The first was finding common denominators and then dividing the numerators. The second was multiplying the dividend by the denominator of the divisor. Then divide the result by the numerator of the divisor.

Both algorithms consistently give the correct answer. We looked for patterns. Then we made sure those patterns worked for all division with fractions problems.

Common Core Standards for Mathematical Practice

MP8 Look for and express regularity in repeated reasoning.

- What other Mathematical Practices can you identify in Hector's reasoning?
- Describe a Mathematical Practice that you and your classmates used to solve a different Problem in this Investigation.

Wrapping Up the Operations

4.1 Just the Facts

Fact Families for Addition and Subtraction

In Investigation 1, you wrote addition and subtraction sentences to show calculations you did. For each addition sentence you write, there are related number sentences that show the same information. These sets of number sentences form a related set of facts called a *fact family*.

- How could you write a number sentence showing a relationship among 7, 2, and 9?
- Is there more than one correct number sentence?

Below are two fact families. The family on the left has all values included. The family on the right has a missing value.

	Example 1	Example 2
Addition Sentence	$2 + 3 = 5$	$2 + n = 5$
Related Number Sentences	$3 + 2 = 5$ $5 - 3 = 2$ $5 - 2 = 3$	$n + 2 = 5$ $5 - n = 2$ $5 - 2 = n$

- How are the three additional sentences related to the original sentence?

Common Core State Standards

6.EE.A.2 Write, read, and evaluate expressions in which letters stand for numbers.

6.EE.B.6 Use variables to represent numbers and write expressions when solving a real-world or mathematical problem; understand that a variable can represent an unknown number . . .

6.EE.B.7 Solve real-world and mathematical problems by writing and solving equations of the form $x + p = q$ and $px = q$ for cases in which p, q and x are all nonnegative rational numbers.

You can also create fact families with fractions.

- What number sentences can you write showing a relationship among $\frac{1}{2}$, $\frac{1}{4}$, and $\frac{3}{4}$?

Ravi says that when he is thinking about fact families, he thinks about a picture like a section in Tupelo Township. The parts of the large rectangle represent the *addends*. The entire large rectangle represents the total acreage, or the *sum*.

- The total area of the rectangle below is 42 acres. What number sentence does this model represent?

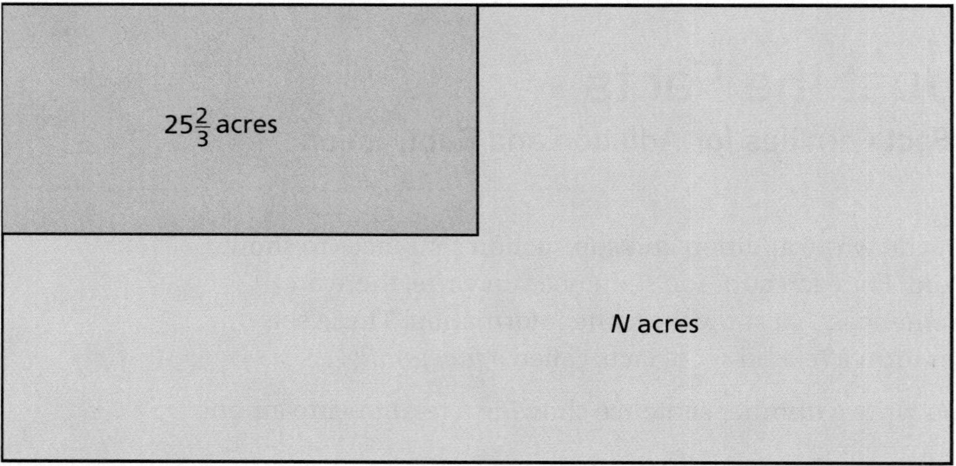

- What are some other ways of writing the relationship between $25\frac{2}{3}$, N, and 42 acres?

The model shows that any sum can be broken down, *or decomposed,* into two (or more) parts. The parts are the addends. In Ravi's model, the total acreage, the sum, is 42 acres. The parts, N acres and $25\frac{2}{3}$ acres, are the addends.

Below are two fact families expressing relationships among fractions.

	Example 1	Example 2
Addition Sentence	$\frac{3}{4}+\frac{1}{8}=\frac{7}{8}$	$\frac{6}{8}+N=\frac{7}{8}$
Related Number Sentences	$\frac{1}{8}+\frac{3}{4}=\frac{7}{8}$ $\frac{7}{8}-\frac{3}{4}=\frac{1}{8}$ $\frac{7}{8}-\frac{1}{8}=\frac{3}{4}$	$N+\frac{6}{8}=\frac{7}{8}$ $\frac{7}{8}-\frac{6}{8}=N$ $\frac{7}{8}-N=\frac{6}{8}$

- How are these fact families different from each other?
- How do you know that the three related sentences below the top row are true?

In Problem 4.1 you will create fact families and use them to find unknown numbers.

Problem 4.1

A For each number sentence, write a complete fact family and find the value of *N*.

1. $\frac{5}{10}-\frac{2}{5}=N$
2. $3\frac{3}{5}+1\frac{2}{3}=N$
3. Describe the relationship between addition and subtraction. Use the fact families in parts (1) and (2) as examples.

B For each number sentence, find the value of *N*.

1. $N+1\frac{2}{3}=5\frac{5}{6}$
2. $\frac{3}{4}+N=\frac{17}{12}$
3. $N-\frac{1}{2}=\frac{3}{8}$
4. How can fact families help you find the value of *N* in parts (1)–(3)?

ACE Homework starts on page 73.

4.2 Multiplication and Division Fact Families

In Problem 4.1 you wrote fact families made up of related addition and subtraction sentences. You can also use fact families to show relationships between multiplication and division.

	Example 1	Example 2
Multiplication Sentence	$4 \times 5 = 20$	$17 \times N = 51$
Related Number Sentences	$5 \times 4 = 20$ $20 \div 5 = 4$ $20 \div 4 = 5$	$N \times 17 = 51$ $51 \div N = 17$ $51 \div 17 = N$

In Problem 4.1, you saw Ravi's rectangular model for adding area. For multiplication, Ravi uses words instead of a model to help him decide on the correct rearrangements. Any multiplication sentence, whether involving fractions or whole numbers, can be written in the form below.

$$\text{(factor 1)} \times \text{(factor 2)} = \text{product}$$

- How might you rearrange the sentence above but still keep the same relationship between factor 1, factor 2, and the product?
- How might you rearrange the sentence $\frac{2}{3} \times N = \frac{1}{2}$ to complete the following table?

	Example 1	Example 2
Multiplication Sentence	$\frac{1}{2} \times \frac{1}{3} = \frac{1}{6}$	$\frac{2}{3} \times N = \frac{1}{2}$
Related Number Sentences	$\frac{1}{3} \times \frac{1}{2} = \frac{1}{6}$ $\frac{1}{6} \div \frac{1}{3} = \frac{1}{2}$ $\frac{1}{6} \div \frac{1}{2} = \frac{1}{3}$	

- In Example 2 in the table above, which rearrangement is most helpful for finding the value of N?

Problem 4.2

Now it is your turn to write fact families.

A Write a complete fact family for each of the following sentences.

1. $\frac{2}{3} \times \frac{1}{5} = \frac{2}{15}$
2. $\frac{3}{4} \times \frac{5}{8} = \frac{15}{32}$
3. $\frac{9}{40} \div \frac{3}{5} = \frac{3}{8}$
4. $\frac{4}{15} \div \frac{2}{5} = \frac{2}{3}$

B Write a complete fact family for each of the following equations. Use your fact family to find the value of N.

1. $\frac{3}{8} \times N = \frac{21}{80}$
2. $\frac{2}{3} \times N = \frac{10}{15}$
3. $1 \div N = \frac{2}{3}$
4. $\frac{8}{15} \div N = \frac{2}{3}$

C Marla says she can use the idea of *decomposing* a product to find the unknown factor, N, in $15 = 2 \times N$. She rearranges this multiplication sentence as the division sentence $15 \div 2 = N$. Does Marla's strategy work? Explain why or why not.

D Below are sets of three numbers. Some of these sets can be related using addition and subtraction. Some can be related using multiplication and division. For each set, identify what the relation is. Then write a complete fact family.

1. $\frac{3}{5}, \frac{1}{3}, \frac{14}{15}$
2. $\frac{3}{4}, \frac{4}{3}, 1$
3. $1\frac{1}{2}, 2\frac{2}{3}, 4\frac{1}{6}$
4. $\frac{3}{2}, 3, \frac{9}{2}$

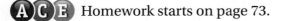

ACE Homework starts on page 73.

4.3 Becoming an Operations Sleuth

In *Let's Be Rational* you have revisited and deepened your skills with the operations addition, subtraction, multiplication, and division. In the real world, problems do not come with labels saying *add, subtract, multiply,* or *divide.* You need to use your mathematics knowledge to identify which operation will be helpful to solve a problem.

Think about the operations you would use in the following situations.

The sixth-grade class is taking a field trip to the state capital. There are 389 students in the sixth grade, but 29 did not get the permission slip signed by their parents. The principal needs to know how many sixth-grade students have permission to go on the field trip.

A varsity softball team has 15 players. The junior varsity team has 10 players. The fan club is buying the teams new uniforms. The fan club wants to know how many uniforms they need to buy.

There are 360 students going on a field trip. Each school bus carries 30 students. The school office needs to know how many buses to send.

The school auditorium has 30 rows of 50 seats each. You want to find out how many seats are in the auditorium.

- Which situations require you to add? Which require you to subtract?
- Which require you to multiply? Which require you to divide?
- How do you know?

In Problem 4.3 you will examine situations that require computations with fractions. In each case your first task is to determine what operations will help you solve the problem.

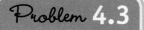

Problem 4.3

For each of the Questions below, do the following.

- Decide which operation you need to find an answer. Explain how you identified the operation.
- When you use more than one operation, explain the order in which you use them.
- Write the number sentence(s) you use.
- Find the answer.

A Sammy the turtle can walk $\frac{1}{8}$ of a mile in an hour. How many hours will it take him to walk $1\frac{1}{4}$ miles?

B Jimarcus plans to build a fence $5\frac{1}{3}$ yards long at the back of his garden. How many $\frac{2}{3}$-yard sections of fence will he need?

C Sasha bought $3\frac{1}{2}$ pints of blueberries to make jelly. She ate $\frac{3}{4}$ of a pint of berries on her way home. How many pints of berries does she have left to make jelly?

D Judi uses $2\frac{3}{4}$ pounds of potatoes every week. How many pounds of potatoes does she use in $3\frac{1}{2}$ weeks?

continued on the next page >

Problem 4.3 continued

E At a bake sale, Leslie sold $2\frac{1}{2}$ dozen sweet rolls. Christie sold sweet rolls but did not keep track of what she sold. She started with 5 dozen sweet rolls and had $1\frac{2}{3}$ dozen left at the end of the sale. Who sold more sweet rolls? How many more did she sell?

F Raymar ate $\frac{1}{4}$ of a pan of brownies. His brother Kalen ate $\frac{1}{4}$ of the rest of the pan of brownies. What part of the whole pan did Kalen eat?

G Mrs. Larnell is making snack packs for a class picnic. She puts $\frac{1}{4}$ pound of apples, $\frac{1}{8}$ pound of nut mix, and $\frac{1}{16}$ pound of chocolate in each student's pack. There are 24 students in the class. What is the total weight of the snack packs? Is there more than one way to solve this problem?

H A grandmother is making clothes for her three granddaughters. She will make a jacket and one other item for each granddaughter. The three other items will be exactly the same. A jacket takes $1\frac{5}{8}$ yards of fabric. She has ten yards of material in all. She is trying to figure out how much fabric she has for each of the three extra items.

Let N represent the fabric needed for one extra item. Explain why each of the sentences below does or does not describe the situation. (More than one sentence may apply.)

1. $3\left(1\frac{5}{8} + N\right) = 10$
2. $10 - 4\frac{7}{8} = 3N$
3. $3 \times 1\frac{5}{8} + N = 10$
4. $10 \div 1\frac{5}{8} = N$

ACE Homework starts on page 73.

Applications

For each of Exercises 1–4, write a complete fact family.

1. $\frac{1}{16} + \frac{1}{12} = N$
2. $\frac{5}{4} - \frac{4}{5} = N$
3. $N - 1\frac{1}{3} = 2\frac{2}{3}$
4. $N + \frac{4}{3} = \frac{1}{3}$

For Exercises 5–10, find the value for *N* that makes each number sentence true.

5. $\frac{2}{3} + \frac{3}{4} = N$
6. $\frac{3}{4} + N = \frac{4}{5}$
7. $N - \frac{3}{5} = \frac{1}{4}$
8. $\frac{2}{2} - \frac{2}{4} = N$
9. $\frac{3}{8} - N = \frac{1}{4}$
10. $\frac{3}{4} + N = \frac{5}{8}$

11. Find the value for m that makes this number sentence true:
$\frac{1}{2} + \frac{9}{10} + m = 2.$

12. Find values for m and n that make this number sentence true:
$\frac{1}{2} + \frac{9}{10} + m + n = 2.$

13. Find the value for m that makes this number sentence true:
$\frac{1}{2} + \frac{9}{10} = 2 - m.$

For Exercises 14 and 15, write a complete multiplication and division fact family for the operation given.

14. $\frac{2}{3} \times \frac{5}{7} = \frac{10}{21}$
15. $\frac{3}{4} \div 1\frac{1}{2} = \frac{1}{2}$

Solve Exercises 16–21.

16. $N \times \frac{1}{5} = \frac{2}{15}$

17. $N \div \frac{1}{5} = \frac{2}{3}$

18. $\frac{1}{2} \times N = \frac{1}{3}$

19. $\frac{1}{5} \div N = \frac{1}{3}$

20. $1\frac{3}{4} \div N = \frac{1}{4}$

21. $2\frac{2}{3} \div N = 8$

22. Find the value for m that makes each number sentence true.

a. $\frac{2}{3} \times \frac{4}{5} \times m = \frac{1}{3}$

b. $\frac{4}{5} \times \frac{2}{3} \times m = \frac{1}{3}$

c. $\frac{2}{3} \times \frac{4}{5} = \frac{1}{3} \div m$

23. Gregory is building a pen for his new puppy. He needs the pen to be $9\frac{1}{2}$ feet by $6\frac{3}{4}$ feet. How many feet of fencing does he need?

24. Sam goes to the market to buy hamburger for a cookout. He buys $3\frac{3}{4}$ pounds of hamburger. How many $\frac{1}{4}$-pound patties can he make?

25. a. Kalisha made two dozen large buns. She ate $\frac{1}{2}$ of a bun and gave her mother and father one each. How many buns does she have left?

b. She is going to cut the remaining buns into thirds for a party. How many $\frac{1}{3}$-size buns will she have?

26. Eun Mi raked $\frac{1}{3}$ of her mother's lawn. Her brother, Yeping, raked $\frac{1}{3}$ of the rest of the lawn. What part of the whole lawn still needs raking?

27. Monday through Friday a grocery store buys $\frac{2}{3}$ bushel of apples per day from a local grower. Saturday the grocer buys $1\frac{1}{3}$ bushels of apples. If the grocer buys apples for four weeks, how many bushels of apples does he buy?

28. Kalin walks at a steady rate of $3\frac{2}{3}$ miles per hour. The beach is $4\frac{1}{4}$ miles from his home. How long will it take Kalin to walk from his home to the beach and back to his home?

Connections

29. **a.** Find the value for N that makes this number sentence true:
$\left(\frac{1}{4} + \frac{1}{3}\right)N = \frac{1}{2}$.

b. Find the value for N that makes this number sentence true:
$\frac{1}{4} + \frac{1}{3}N = \frac{1}{2}$.

c. Why are the correct answers for part (a) and part (b) different from each other?

For Exercises 30–38, find each missing number.

30. $2 \times ■ = 1$

31. $\frac{1}{2} \times ■ = 1$

32. $3 \times ■ = 1$

33. $\frac{1}{3} \times ■ = 1$

34. $■ \times \frac{2}{3} = 1$

35. $\frac{3}{4} \times ■ = 1$

36. $■ \times \frac{5}{2} = 1$

37. $1\frac{1}{4} \times ■ = 1$

38. $\frac{7}{12} \times ■ = 1$

For Exercises 39–41, find the missing numbers in each pair of number sentences. What is the relationship between each pair of numbers?

39. $3 \div ■ = 9$
$3 \times ■ = 9$

40. $3 \div ■ = 12$
$3 \times ■ = 12$

41. $2\frac{1}{2} \div ■ = 5$
$2\frac{1}{2} \times ■ = 5$

For Exercises 42–43, estimate which sum or difference is greater. Then compute the answers to compare with your estimates. Show your work.

42. $\frac{1}{8} + \frac{5}{6}$ or $\frac{1}{6} + \frac{5}{8}$

43. $\frac{5}{6} - \frac{1}{8}$ or $\frac{5}{8} - \frac{1}{6}$

44. Find the value for N that makes this number sentence true:
$3 \times \left(N + \frac{1}{3}\right) = 2$

45. Find the value for N that makes this number sentence true:
$\left(N + \frac{1}{2}\right) \times 1\frac{1}{2} = 2\frac{1}{4}$

46. In the number sentence below, find values for m and n that make the sum exactly 3.

$$\frac{5}{8} + \frac{1}{4} + \frac{2}{3} + m + n = 3$$

Extensions

For Exercises 47–50, find the value of N that makes each number sentence true.

47. $\frac{1}{2} + N = \frac{1}{2}$

48. $\frac{1}{2} - N = \frac{1}{2}$

49. $\frac{1}{2} \times N = \frac{1}{2}$

50. $\frac{1}{2} \div N = \frac{1}{2}$

51. Mathematicians call the number 0 the *additive identity*. They call the number 1 the *multiplicative identity*. Based on your work in Exercises 47–50, what do you think *identity* means?

For Exercises 52–55, find the value of N that makes each number sentence true.

52. $\frac{1}{2} + N = 0$

53. $\frac{2}{3} + N = 0$

54. $\frac{1}{2} \times N = 1$

55. $\frac{2}{3} \times N = 1$

56. Mathematicians have a special name for each value of N you found in Exercises 52–55. Each N is the additive or multiplicative *inverse* of the number you started with.

- An *additive inverse* is the number you add to another number to get 0.
- A *multiplicative inverse* is the number you multiply by another number to get 1.

a. Does every number have an additive inverse?

b. Does every number have a multiplicative inverse?

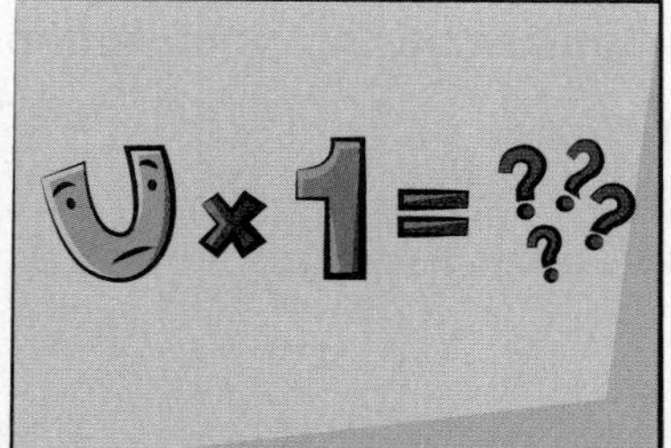

Mathematical Reflections

In this Investigation, you explored relationships among addition, subtraction, multiplication and division. The following questions will help you summarize what you have learned.

Think about these questions. Discuss your ideas with other students and your teacher. Then write a summary of your findings in your notebook.

1. **How** do you decide which operation to use when you are solving a problem?
2. **How** is the relationship between addition and subtraction like the relationship between multiplication and division? **How** is it different?
3. While working with fact families, you thought about *decomposing* numbers.
   a. **What** does it mean to decompose a number?
   b. **How** do fact families help you figure out the value for N in a sentence such as $N \div 2\frac{1}{2} = 1\frac{1}{4}$?

Common Core Mathematical Practices

As you worked on the Problems in this Investigation, you used prior knowledge to make sense of them. You also applied Mathematical Practices to solve the Problems. Think back over your work, the ways you thought about the Problems, and how you used Mathematical Practices.

Tori described her thoughts in the following way:

In Problem 4.3, we had to figure out whether to add, subtract, multiply, or divide. Sometimes we used a combination of operations. We had to read each problem really carefully.

Sometimes we drew a picture to represent what the problem was asking. This helped us figure out which operation to use. For example, if the problem called for combining quantities, we used addition.

This was a good way to end because in real life, you don't get told which operation to use. You need to figure it out.

Common Core Standards for Mathematical Practice
MP2 Reason abstractly and quantitatively.

- What other Mathematical Practices can you identify in Tori's reasoning?
- Describe a Mathematical Practice that you and your classmates used to solve a different Problem in this Investigation.

Looking Back

During this Unit, you developed strategies for estimating and computing with fractions and mixed numbers. You learned how to determine which situations call for which operations when working with fractions and mixed numbers. You developed algorithms for adding, subtracting, multiplying, and dividing fractions. You learned how to solve problems with fractions. Use what you have learned to solve the following examples.

Use Your Understanding: Fraction Operations

1. The Scoop Shop sells many types of nuts. Lily asks for this mix:
   - $\frac{1}{2}$ pound peanuts
   - $\frac{1}{6}$ pound hazelnuts
   - $\frac{1}{3}$ pound almonds
   - $\frac{3}{4}$ pound cashews
   - $\frac{1}{4}$ pound pecans

   a. Mixed nuts cost \$5.00 per pound. What is Lily's bill?
   b. What fraction of the mix does each type of nut represent?
   c. Diego does not like cashews, so he asks for Lily's mix without the cashews. What is Diego's bill?
   d. Taisha is making small bowls of nuts for a party. Each bowl can hold $\frac{1}{4}$ cup of nuts. Taisha has $3\frac{3}{8}$ cups of nuts. How many full bowls can she make?

2. Shaquille likes dried fruit. He wants a mix of peaches, cherries, pineapple chunks, and apple rings. The following chart shows how much The Scoop Shop has of each fruit. It also shows how much of each fruit Shaquille buys.

The Scoop Shop's Stock	Shaquille's Order
$1\frac{1}{2}$ pounds dried peaches	$\frac{1}{3}$ of the stock
$\frac{4}{5}$ pound dried cherries	$\frac{1}{2}$ of the stock
$\frac{3}{4}$ pound dried pineapple chunks	$\frac{2}{3}$ of the stock
$2\frac{1}{4}$ pounds dried apple rings	$\frac{3}{5}$ of the stock

a. How many pounds of dried fruit does Shaquille buy?

b. Dried fruit costs $6.00 per pound. What is Shaquille's bill?

Explain Your Reasoning

When you solve a problem or make a decision, it is important to be able to support each step of your reasoning.

3. What operations did you use to calculate Lily's bill?
4. How did you find the fraction of Lily's mix that each type of nut represented?
5. Jacob says that $4 \div \frac{1}{3} = 12$ and $4 \div \frac{2}{3} = 6$. Why is the answer in the second number sentence half of the answer in the first number sentence?
6. Use the following problems to show the steps involved in the algorithms for each operation on fractions. Be prepared to explain your reasoning.

   a. $\frac{5}{6} + \frac{1}{4}$ b. $\frac{3}{4} - \frac{2}{3}$ c. $\frac{2}{5} \times \frac{3}{8}$ d. $\frac{3}{8} \div \frac{3}{4}$

English / Spanish Glossary

A

algorithm A set of rules for performing a procedure. Mathematicians invent algorithms that are useful in many kinds of situations. Some examples of algorithms are the rules for long division or the rules for adding two fractions.

To add two fractions, first change them to equivalent fractions with the same denominator. Then add the numerators and put the sum over the common denominator.

algoritmo Un conjunto de reglas para realizar un procedimiento. Los matemáticos inventan algoritmos que son útiles en muchos tipos de situaciones. Algunos ejemplos de algoritmos son las reglas para una división larga o las reglas para sumar dos fracciones. El siguiente es un algoritmo escrito por un estudiante de un grado intermedio.

Para sumar dos fracciones, primero transfórmalas en fracciones equivalentes con el mismo denominador. Luego suma los numeradores y coloca la suma sobre el denominador común.

B

benchmark A reference number that can be used to estimate the size of other numbers. For work with fractions, 0, $\frac{1}{2}$, and 1 are good benchmarks. We often estimate fractions or decimals with benchmarks because it is easier to do arithmetic with them, and estimates often give enough accuracy for the situation. For example, many fractions and decimals—such as $\frac{37}{50}$, $\frac{5}{8}$, 0.43, and 0.55—can be thought of as being close to $\frac{1}{2}$. You might say $\frac{5}{8}$ is between $\frac{1}{2}$ and 1 but closer to $\frac{1}{2}$, so you can estimate $\frac{5}{8}$ to be about $\frac{1}{2}$. We also use benchmarks to help compare fractions and decimals. For example, we could say that $\frac{5}{8}$ is greater than 0.43 because $\frac{5}{8}$ is greater than $\frac{1}{2}$ and 0.43 is less than $\frac{1}{2}$.

punto de referencia Un número “bueno” que se puede usar para estimar el tamaño de otros números. Para trabajar con fracciones, 0, $\frac{1}{2}$ y 1 son buenos puntos de referencia. Por lo general estimamos fracciones o decimales con puntos de referencia porque nos resulta más fácil hacer cálculos aritméticos con ellos, y las estimaciones suelen ser bastante exactas para la situación. Por ejemplo, muchas fracciones y decimales, como por ejemplo $\frac{37}{50}$, $\frac{5}{8}$, 0.43 y 0.55, se pueden considerar como cercanos a $\frac{1}{2}$. Se podría decir que $\frac{5}{8}$ está entre $\frac{1}{2}$ y 1, pero más cerca de $\frac{1}{2}$, por lo que se puede estimar que $\frac{5}{8}$ es alrededor de $\frac{1}{2}$. También usamos puntos de referencia para ayudarnos a comparar fracciones. Por ejemplo, podríamos decir que $\frac{5}{8}$ es mayor que 0.43, porque $\frac{5}{8}$ es mayor que $\frac{1}{2}$ y 0.43 es menor que $\frac{1}{2}$.

E

equivalent fractions Fractions that are equal in value, but may have different numerators and denominators. For example, $\frac{2}{3}$ and $\frac{14}{21}$ are equivalent fractions. The shaded part of this rectangle represents both $\frac{2}{3}$ and $\frac{14}{21}$.

fracciones equivalentes Fracciones de igual valor, que pueden tener diferentes numeradores y denominadores. Por ejemplo, $\frac{2}{3}$ y $\frac{14}{21}$ son fracciones equivalentes. La parte sombreada de este rectángulo representa tanto $\frac{2}{3}$ como $\frac{14}{21}$.

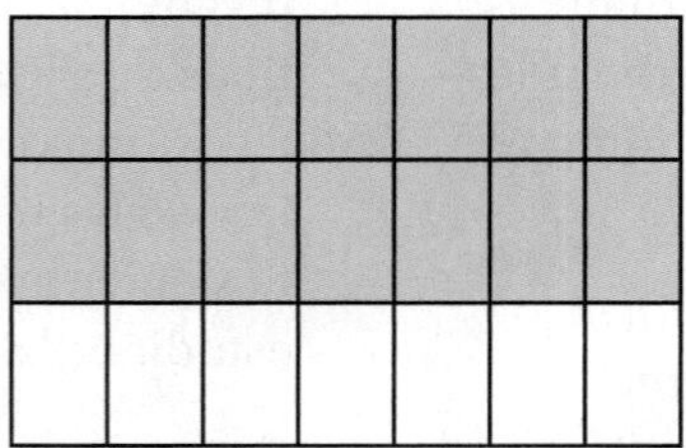

explain Academic Vocabulary To give facts and details that make an idea easier to understand. Explaining can involve a written summary supported by a diagram, chart, table, or a combination of these.

related terms *analyze, clarify, describe, justify, tell*

sample Explain why the answer to $12 \div \frac{3}{4}$ is equal to one third of the answer to $12 \div \frac{1}{4}$.

Because $\frac{3}{4} = 3 \times \frac{1}{4}$, it takes three $\frac{1}{4}$s to make every $\frac{3}{4}$. There are forty-eight $\frac{1}{4}$s in 12, but there are only sixteen $\frac{3}{4}$s in 12.

explicar Vocabulario académico Dar datos y detalles que hacen que una idea sea más fácil de comprender. Explicar puede incluir un resumen escrito apoyado por un diagrama, una gráfica, una tabla o una combinación de éstos.

términos relacionados *analizar, aclarar, describir, justificar, decir*

ejemplo Explica por qué el resultado de $12 \div \frac{3}{4}$ es igual a un tercio del resultado de $12 \div \frac{1}{4}$.

Porque $\frac{3}{4} = 3 \times \frac{1}{4}$, se requieren tres $\frac{1}{4}$ para formar cada $\frac{3}{4}$. Hay cuarenta y ocho $\frac{1}{4}$ en 12, pero sólo hay dieciséis $\frac{3}{4}$ en 12.

fact family A set of related addition–subtraction sentences or multiplication–division sentences. For example, the set of numbers, 3, 5, and 15, is part of this multiplication–division fact family:

$3 \times 5 = 15$ $5 \times 3 = 15$

$15 \div 5 = 3$ $15 \div 3 = 5$

If you have one fact from a family, you can use the addition–subtraction or multiplication–division relationship to write the three related facts that are also part of the family. For example, with $2 + 3 = 5$, you can use the relationship between addition and subtraction to write the related number sentences $3 + 2 = 5$, $5 - 3 = 2$, and $5 - 2 = 3$.

familia de operaciones Conjunto de oraciones relacionadas de suma y resta o de multiplicación y división. Por ejemplo, los números 3, 5 y 15, son parte de esta familia de operaciones de multiplicación y división:

$3 \times 5 = 15$ $5 \times 3 = 15$

$15 \div 5 = 3$ $15 \div 3 = 5$

Si conoces una operación de una familia de operaciones, puedes usar la relación entre la suma y la resta, y entre la multiplicación y la división, para escribir las otras tres operaciones relacionadas que son parte de esa familia. Por ejemplo, con $2 + 3 = 5$, puedes usar la relación entre la suma y la resta para escribir las oraciones numéricas relacionadas $3 + 2 = 5$, $5-3 = 2$ y $5 - 2 = 3$.

M

model Academic Vocabulary To represent a situation using pictures, diagrams, number sentences, or experiments.

related terms *represent, demonstrate*

sample Yolanda has one half of an apple pie. She eats one third of the half of a pie. Model this situation using a number sentence or a picture.

I can write one third as $\frac{1}{3}$ and one half as $\frac{1}{2}$, so one third of one half can be written as $\frac{1}{3} \times \frac{1}{2}$. Because $\frac{1}{3} \times \frac{1}{2} = \frac{1}{6}$, she eats $\frac{1}{6}$ of the entire pie.

I can also fold a whole fraction strip into halves, then fold each half into thirds.

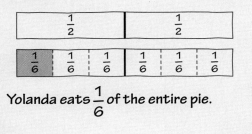

$\frac{1}{2}$			$\frac{1}{2}$		
$\frac{1}{6}$	$\frac{1}{6}$	$\frac{1}{6}$	$\frac{1}{6}$	$\frac{1}{6}$	$\frac{1}{6}$

Yolanda eats $\frac{1}{6}$ of the entire pie.

demostrar Vocabulario académico Representar una situación con dibujos, diagramas, oraciones numéricas o experimentos.

término relacionado *representar*

ejemplo Yolanda tiene la mitad de una tarta de manzana. Se come un tercio de la mitad de la tarta. Demuestra esta situación con una oración numérica o un dibujo.

Puedo escribir un tercio como $\frac{1}{3}$ y la mitad como $\frac{1}{2}$, así que un tercio de una mitad puede escribirse como $\frac{1}{3} \times \frac{1}{2}$. Debido a que $\frac{1}{3} \times \frac{1}{2} = \frac{1}{6}$, ella se come $\frac{1}{6}$ de la tarta entera.

También puedo doblar una tira de fracciones por el medio para obtener mitades y doblar cada mitad en tres tercios.

$\frac{1}{2}$			$\frac{1}{2}$		
$\frac{1}{6}$	$\frac{1}{6}$	$\frac{1}{6}$	$\frac{1}{6}$	$\frac{1}{6}$	$\frac{1}{6}$

Yolanda se come $\frac{1}{6}$ de la tarta entera.

N

number sentence A mathematical statement that gives the relationship between two expressions that are composed of numbers and operation signs. For example, $3 + 2 = 5$ and $6 \times 2 > 10$ are number sentences; $3 + 2$, 5, 6×2, and 10 are expressions.

oración numérica Enunciado matemático que describe la relación entre dos expresiones compuestas por números y signos de operaciones. Por ejemplo, $3 + 2 = 5$ y $6 \times 2 > 10$ son oraciones numéricas; $3 + 2$, 5, 6×2 y 10 son expresiones.

O

overestimate To make an estimate that is slightly greater than the actual value.

estimación por exceso Una estimación que es un poco mayor que el valor real.

R

reason Academic Vocabulary To think through using facts and information.

related terms *think, examine, logic*

sample To find the number of $\frac{1}{2}$-cup servings in 6 cups, Jenni says it is necessary to multiply 6 by $\frac{1}{2}$. Zach says that 6 must be divided by $\frac{1}{2}$ to find the number of servings. Do you agree with Jenni or Zach? Explain how you reasoned.

I agree with Zach because you want to know how many halves there are in 6. This question is answered by division: $6 \div \frac{1}{2} = 12$. Multiplying 6 by $\frac{1}{2}$ separates it into 2 equal parts of 3 each. That is not what is asked for in the question.

razonar Vocabulario académico Pensar algo con cuidado usando operaciones e información.

términos relacionados *pensar, examinar, lógico*

ejemplo Para hallar el número de porciones de $\frac{1}{2}$ taza que hay en 6 tazas, Jenni dice que se debe multiplicar 6 por $\frac{1}{2}$. Zach dice que hay que dividir 6 por $\frac{1}{2}$ para hallar el número de porciones. ¿Estás de acuerdo con Jenni o con Zach? Explica tu razonamiento.

Estoy de acuerdo con Zach porque se desea saber cuántas mitades hay en 6. Esta pregunta se responde usando la división: $6 \div \frac{1}{2} = 12$. Multiplicar 6 por $\frac{1}{2}$ lo separa en 2 partes iguales de 3 cada una. Esto no es lo que se pide en la pregunta.

recall Academic Vocabulary To remember a fact quickly.

related terms *remember, recognize*

sample Mateo wants to add 0.3 to $\frac{1}{2}$. What fact can you recall about $\frac{1}{2}$ or 0.3 that will help him find the sum? Explain.

I recall that $\frac{1}{2}$ is equivalent to the decimal 0.5. When both numbers are in decimal form, they can be added easily. Mateo can add 0.5 + 0.3 to get 0.8.

I also recall that 0.3 is the same as $\frac{3}{10}$ and $\frac{1}{2}$ is equivalent to $\frac{5}{10}$. Mateo can add $\frac{3}{10} + \frac{5}{10}$ to get $\frac{8}{10}$ which is the same as 0.8.

recordar Vocabulario académico Acordarse de una operación rápidamente.

términus relacionados *acordarse, reconocer*

ejemplo Mateo quiere sumar 0.3 y $\frac{1}{2}$. ¿Qué operación con $\frac{1}{2}$ ó 0.3 puedes recordar para ayudarlo a hallar la suma? Explica tu respuesta.

Recuerdo que $\frac{1}{2}$ es equivalente al número decimal 0.5. Cuando ambos números están en forma decimal, pueden sumarse con facilidad. Mateo puede sumar 0.5 + 0.3 para obtener 0.8.

También recuerdo que 0.3 igual $\frac{3}{10}$ y $\frac{1}{2}$ es equivalente a $\frac{5}{10}$. Mateo puede sumar $\frac{3}{10} + \frac{5}{10}$ para obtener $\frac{8}{10}$, que es igual a 0.8.

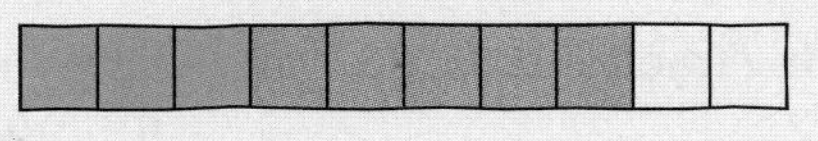

reciprocal A factor by which you multiply a given number so that their product is 1. For example, $\frac{3}{5}$ is the reciprocal of $\frac{5}{3}$, and $\frac{5}{3}$ is the reciprocal of $\frac{3}{5}$ because $\frac{3}{5} \times \frac{5}{3} = 1$. Note that the reciprocal of $1\frac{2}{3}$ is $\frac{3}{5}$ because $1\frac{2}{3} \times \frac{3}{5} = 1$.

recíproco Un factor por el cual multiplicas un dado de manera que su producto sea 1. Por ejemplo, $\frac{3}{5}$ es el recíproco de $\frac{5}{3}$, y $\frac{5}{3}$ es el recíproco de $\frac{3}{5}$, porque $\frac{3}{5} \times \frac{5}{3} = 1$. Observa que el recíproco de $1\frac{2}{3}$ es $\frac{3}{5}$, porque $1\frac{2}{3} \times \frac{3}{5} = 1$.

underestimate To make an estimate that is slightly less than the actual value.

estimación por defecto Una estimación que es un poco menor que el valor real.

Index

Acknowledgments

Cover Design

Three Communication Design, Chicago

Photographs

Photo locators denoted as follows: Top (T), Center (C), Bottom (B), Left (L), Right (R), Background (Bkgd)

002 Serguei Liachenko/Fotolia; **003** Christy Thompson/Shutterstock; **013** Gigra/Fotolia; **040** Serguei Liachenko/Fotolia; **061** ©2001 Hilary B. Price/King Features Syndicate; **074** Photoexpert117/Fotolia.